a

echoesoftranslation

readingbetweentexts

Rainer Nägele

The Johns Hopkins University Press

Baltimore & London

06 05 04 03 02 01 00 99 98 97   5 4 3 2 1

© The Johns Hopkins University Press
All rights reserved. Published 1997
Printed in the United States of America
on acid-free paper

The Johns Hopkins University Press,
2715 North Charles Street, Baltimore,
Maryland 21218-4319

The Johns Hopkins Press Ltd., London

Library of Congress Cataloging-in-
Publication Data will be found at the
end of this book.

A catalog record of this book is available from the British Library.

ISBN 0-8018-5545-4

Contents

Author's Note

References to Baudelaire's works are cited from:

Charles Baudelaire. *Oeuvres complètes*. Bibliothèque de la Pléiade. Paris: Gallimard, 1976.

References to Benjamin's works are cited by volume and page from:

Walter Benjamin. *Gesammelte Schriften*. Edited by Rolf Tiedemann and Hermann Schweppenhäuser. Frankfurt am Main: Suhrkamp, 1980– .

References to Freud are cited from:

Sigmund Freud. *Studienausgabe*. Frankfurt am Main: S. Fischer, 1969–75.

References to Hölderlin's works are cited according to the two major editions:

FA = Freidrich Hölderlin. *Sämtliche Werke. Frankdurter Ausgabe*. Frankfurt am Main: Roter Stern, 1979– .

StA = Friedrich Hölderlin. *Sämtliche Werke*. Große Stuttarter Ausgabe. Stuttgart: Kohlhammer, 1943–1974.

References to Nietzsche are cited from:

Friedrich Nietzsche. *Sämtliche Werke. Kritische Studienausgabe*. Munich: Deutscher Taschenbuchverlag, 1980.

All translations, if not otherwise indicated, are my own.

ans

t

Introduction

Reading between Texts

Tous les échos de la mémoire, si on pouvait les réveiller simultanément, formeraient un concert, agréable ou douloureux, mais logique et sans dissonances.—Charles Baudelaire

La confusion des langues n'est plus une punition, le sujet accède à la jouissance par la cohabitation des langages, *qui travaillent côte à côte:* le texte de plaisir, c'est Babel heureuse.—Roland Barthes

Das Fremdeste paarend und das Nächste trennend. —Friedrich Nietzsche

A confusion of languages already meets the eye in the epigraphs and continues in the text in yet another language. Foreign quotations and words are scattered throughout these essays. This could be seen as an annoying gesture, a vain display of erudition. If it were a claim for the superiority of one language over another, it would be even more annoying and inherently false, as if to say German or Greek, for example, are so much closer to truth than English. It happens that German is almost (not quite) my native language. I say only "almost" because German is not the tongue of my mother, my father, or my childhood, but it is the native language of my reading and writing. It happened that Greek, in the enigmatic difference of its writing, appeared as the obscure object of desire to me almost at the same time that I became intoxicated by the sounds of German poetry, reciting Goethe and Hölderlin, my first discoveries in cheap paperback editions, to myself for hours, translating the pleasures of the written into the pleasures of the tongue and ear. Almost at the same time the first sounds of French were transmitted to me; a few years later, I discovered through Baudelaire and Rimbaud a poetry that was very different from that of Goethe and Hölderlin, but it produced a lasting impact, almost a shock, which lingers on like the shock of a first love.

The following essays are echoes of this kind of impact. It happened. It happened to happen in these particular, specific configurations. These configurations are invoked here by a writing that circles again and again around the same texts, in an attempt to register what happened. Such writing is already echo. Each encounter with any specific language or with any specific text is already determined by a structure of resonance. It is the memory of the first and singular encounter, not with any language but with Language.

It is the task of writing, as it is understood here, to register what happened to happen, that is, to register the resonances that constitute every moment of history as a dialectical configuration of the singular with a repetition. To register: as, for example, Kafka's diary registers the beginning of the First World War: "Deutschland hat Rußland den Krieg erklärt. —Nachmittag Schwimmschule" [Germany has declared war on Russia. —Afternoon swimming school].[1] The entry has been interpreted as a disturbing retreat from the world into the private sphere, as a symptom of Kafka's alienation from the world. But no guilt-ridden reflection could match the diagnostic precision of the juxtaposition and the dash that register an objective historical structure in the relationship between private and public sphere.

Where such a registration has taken place and offers itself as a gift to be read, the work of reading and writing can begin and continue ever anew. The singularity of a dash and the juxtaposition of two sentences that mark two heterogeneous events are the data and the stuff that history is made of: not the events in their abstract infinity but the traces of their impact.

If writing is a reading of the traces of an impact, it must begin where a trace is felt as an impact. It has to be the result of an impact that resonates through writing and dictates its rhythm. Neither writing nor political analysis can emerge from empathy and public concern. The latter are the sites of a misplaced moralization that blocks analysis on every level and provides the fertile ground for any rhetorical seduction that appeals to resentment.

To begin where a trace is felt as an impact, to posit this beginning against any gesture of empathy seems to reduce writing to utter subjectivism. Yet the critique of *empathy*, the term I use here as an equivalent of the German word *Einfühlung*, permeates the writings of modernism and is at the center of such different writers as Brecht and Benjamin, whose writing is remote from any gesture of subjectivism. As I understand it here, empathy translates the German *Einfühlung*, "feeling oneself into" another person or another time, projecting oneself into the interiority of another, or absorbing the other into oneself. It is not the opposite of self-indulgent narcissism but rather its complement.

To begin where a trace is felt as an impact is in all its idiosyncratic singularity the first move of a turning to the world that is constituted by such singularities. This beginning comes at the end of a long process; the process has to be completed again and again in order for the beginning to begin ever anew. This is not a new insight. It has been formulated in many ways, and, more important, it is the distinguishing mark of any genuine writing, writing that emerges from a radical involvement and engagement with the singularities of its experience. The encounter with such writing can produce new experience and writing again. Writing is no longer conceived as 'primary' or 'secondary': writing is that which has worked its way through the encounters given to it. This is true of Hölderlin's poetic language emerging in its most powerful shape from an intense and violent engagement with Pindar and Sophocles, as much as it is true of Benjamin's philosophical, essayistic, and political writing, shaped by the ever renewed encounter with specific moments of the philosophical and literary tradition. These encounters are not defined by influence or by intellectual history and *Geistesgeschichte*. These writings are formed by the resonances produced in the echo chambers of language where events are shaped in the configurations of experience.

If the following essays return insistently (as does all of my writing) to the same texts—to Hölderlin, Baudelaire, Benjamin, Kafka, Freud above all—it is because these texts have become for me testimonies of writing. It is this mode of writing, not any particular content of knowledge provided, which allows and demands the ever renewed return. It does not really matter which writing one chooses, as long as it is a writing that bears the marks of genuine writing. And then one does not choose it; one is chosen by it.

The texts that happen to resonate throughout the essays of this book are shaped by certain common traits and specific ways of responding to these traits. As far as they are historically and geographically part of a tradition of European modernism, they are a response to and a break with specific traits that shaped European romanticism. At the center of romanticism is a figure of departure and return, the shaping structure of romantic narratives. Its philosophical counterpart is the centrality of self-reflection; beyond or beneath the self-reflective philosophical consciousness, the figure also structures the unconscious ideological patterns of self and other. It is most virulent in European anti-Semitism, brought to partial consciousness in Hegel's early writings, when the radical otherness of the Jewish spirit is attributed to an originary leave-taking without return, in opposition to the Christian-romantic spirit and its specular other, the Greek spirit.

Taking leave of romanticism, Baudelaire invokes the counterfigure in "Le voyage": "Mais les vrais voyageurs sont ceux-là seuls qui partent / Pour partir" [But the true travelers are only those who leave in order to take leave] (vv. 17–18). In the romantic narrative one takes leave in order to return all the more to one's own.

Reflection constitutes the romantic adventure of consciousness. That adventure is experienced to its limits in Hölderlin's poetry: at this limit, the figure is radically transformed and consciousness is deflected at its apex, when it finds itself "wandering in the midst of the unthinkable," as Hölderlin writes in the notes to the Sophoclean *Antigone*. He continues: "It is a great resource of the secretly working soul that at the highest state of consciousness it evades consciousness. . . . In a high state of consciousness, then, it always compares itself to objects that do not have any consciousness, yet which in their destiny assume the form of consciousness."[2] This deflection and rupture in the movement of (self-)consciousness and reflection is the distinctive mark of the writings of Kafka, Freud, and Benjamin and of a large part of contemporary philosophy.[3] Habermas's symptomatic misconception of Freud's psychoanalysis as self-reflection[4] goes hand in hand with his systematic attempt in *The Philosophical Discourse of Modernity*[5] to separate a clean, reasonable modernity from an anarchistic mad postmodernism.

Freud had recognized very early that self-analysis in the proper sense is impossible. What seemed like a self-analysis was interrupted, and the decisive insight emerged from the caesura: "My self-analysis remains interrupted. I have seen why. I can analyze myself only with objectively gained knowledge (like a stranger), self-analysis in the proper sense is impossible."[6] Analysis is the reading of traces, the listening to a language that can never be reduced to the expression of an individual. This is precisely the point where Benjamin, like Freud, breaks away from psychologism. In an early fragment on psychology, the rupture is posited categorically: "First, there is no psychological [seelische] behavior that is fundamentally and essentially different from corporeal [leiblicher] behavior. . . . The supposed difference that the psychological life of a stranger [fremdes Seelenleben] is given to us, in contrast to our own, only in mediated form through the interpretation of the foreign corporeality [durch Deutung fremder Leiblichkeit] does not exist. . . . Foreign psychological life is perceived, in principle, not differently from one's own; it is not deduced, but is seen in the corporeal that is proper to it as psychological life."[7] This infolding of the psychological into the corporeal shifts the accent from the psychology that dominated the nineteenth century to a physiognomy that reads the world as a graphematic space, constituted by the traits and marks of experience.

The apparent reduction of the soul to the body is not a naive physiologism. As the body of a being that speaks, the human body is permeated by language, and the perceptual world is structured by language. Benjamin thus radically redefines the subject of psychology as "the relation of the human Gestalt to language" (6:66).

This turn, which in fact is a turn away from psychology, is the basis of all of Benjamin's later work. It also defines his distance from romanticism and from any philosophy based on self-consciousness and self-reflection. The move from his dissertation on the concept of critique in romanticism to the book on the German baroque Trauerspiel is the movement of this turn, explicitly marked in the preface as a critique of the romantic concept of truth: "In ihrem Spekulieren nahm die Wahrheit anstelle ihres sprachlichen Charakters den eines reflektierenden Bewußtseins an" [In their speculation, truth assumed the character of a reflecting consciousness instead of its linguistic character] (1:218). Truth is structured like a language: this principle is the center of Benjamin's writing.

The shift from reflecting consciousness to the structure of language is paralleled by a shift from the optical model of reflection and intellectual intuition (*intellektuelle Anschauung*) to an aural model of hearing and listening to resonances, tones, and echoes. The preface to the *Trauerspiel* book replaces the intellectual intuition with an *Urvernehmen*, a primal hearing and receiving, which resonates with *Vernunft* and suggests the reception of truth not as a possession that can be had but as a gift that is given. Like Hölderlin's poetics of alternating tones, Benjamin's conception of philosophy produces a philosophy of tones, or more precisely of tone relations (*tönendes Verhältnis;* 1:218).

Echo is not self-reflective; it is a reflex. These essays attempt to read those reflexes and resonances in the confusion of languages.

The confusion of tongues, "la confusion des langues," is, according to Roland Barthes, no longer a punishment, "n'est plus une punition." No longer: the sentence suggests that it once was, that perhaps until now it has been a punishment. In the conventional reading and translation of the biblical story of Babel, the confusion of languages punishes a human hybris that wants to reach the sky.

There have been other readings, other translations (our insistent coupling of reading and translation suggests reading *as* translation) from the Talmudic commentaries to the present. Roland Barthes's version of a happy Babel, *c'est Babel heureuse,* takes its place among them. It owes its happiness to a kind of subject that finds its pleasure not in the fulfillment of a phantasy of total identity and communal and communicative homogeneity but in difference, for example, in the cohabitation of different languages rather than in their unification. The construction of the tower of Babel was also the phantasy of a global unification of all humanity under one roof and one language. The narrator in Kafka's story "The Construction of the Chinese Wall" suggests a parallel between the constructions of Babel and of China. The gigantic wall around Kafka's China is a work in progress, a process of construction driven by paranoic fears of outside forces and a compulsion to unify the internal heterogeneity of an immense empire.

The work is still in progress, perhaps more ferociously and more paranoically than ever. The tendency to ever larger global structures and the outbreak of ferocious nationalisms are not opposites but two sides of the same compulsion, where the most modern technologies and economic structures enter into a conjunction with the most atavistic dreams. Freud's suggestion that the death drive is the drive for identity and nondifference should be thought through and taken seriously.

But to think it through means first to step back from global statements and to follow instead the movements of real and apparent heterogeneous details that appear in different languages and between them. This involves following the words not only in their syntactical and contextual habitation but in their constellations as they appear in different and variably distant texts, as stars of different galaxies might form a constellation. The image of the constellation comes from Walter Benjamin, whose text on the task of the translator forms a kind of matrix for the following essays.

Benjamin's text also invokes a wall, but one that is broken rather than built in the work of translation: the literalness of a word-by-word translation open an "arcade" in the "wall of syntax" that covers up Language and makes us forget, in the apparent security of sense and meaning, that we *speak* when we speak about things (4:18).

In Kafka's story, small teams of workers work at various points of the immense circumference of the planned wall and complete a piece here and there. But they never manage to complete the whole wall. No matter how intensely the intention to create total enclosure drives the construction, it remains full of gaps. These gaps are cause for fear but also cause for hope: the paranoia of communal and individual identity fears the intrusion of strange "nomads from the north"; the inhabitant of the happy Babel awaits the unexpected. The latter is a potential companion, although not always a dependable one, for Benjamin's materialist historian who sees catastrophe not in the threats of unexpected change but in the status quo.

The resistance of the walls, like the resistance of an adverse wind or the resistance in an analytical session, can also be used against the force of resistance. The figure of the echo is the figure of a transmission through and with the help of resistance. It is a complex figure that cannot be reduced to the simple repetition of a stable entity. The echo rhymes of baroque poetry, for example, break up words into their syllables and produce new meanings with each return of the fractured word. The echoes of the texts that resonate through the following essays reverberate between an unlocalizable origin, appearing only as a void, and shifting pockets of resistance in the form of precariously stabilized and often petrified fragments of meaning.

In the text of our first epigraph, Baudelaire conceives of memory as an echo: "les échos de la mémoire." The echoes of memory figure remembrance not as a reconstruction of the past but as fragments and refractions of loss. The concert of their simultaneous resounding that Baudelaire imagines is a new music. It is a construction with the pieces of destruction, not a reconstruction. Baudelaire's concert of the echoes of memory is part of the poetics of correspondence. The correspondences are also figured as echoes: "Comme de longs échos qui de loin se confondent" [Like long faraway echoes that melt together].[8] Emanating in the form of confused and confusing words from the forest of symbols, these echoes are closer to the tradition of baroque allegory than to the classic-romantic symbol. The latter is formed according to the ideal of the intact body, represented most perfectly in Greek sculpture. Baudelaire's correspondences are not those between intact bodies and things but those between their refracted qualities and fleeting 'essences'—perfumes, colors, and sounds answer each other: "Les parfums, les couleurs et les sons se répondent." This poetic cosmos echoes the baroque cosmos of correspondences between planets, minerals, and the organs of the human body that enters this cosmos only as *disiecta membra*.[9]

What follows is an attempt at a reading of correspondences, thus, in our sense, an allegorical reading, a reading of an intertextual space between texts, between languages. Such a reading corresponds with Nietzsche's precept in our epigraph: "Das Fremdeste paarend und das Nächste trennend" [Coupling the strangest things and separating the most proximate ones]. This reading is first the exercise of a praxis rather than the formulation of a theory of translation or of intertextuality, although the possibility that our meandering readings between texts might open theoretical perspectives is not excluded and is even desired. Theory then might follow these exercises in reading.

Implicitly and by necessity, theory precedes any praxis of reading, but in such a way, we hope, that the praxis of reading will displace any preconceptions, suspend or transform them. A theoretical assumption that precedes these essays and that can be formulated at the outset is a certain distrust of the fetishization of the concept of theory and formulation of theory without regard for the praxis that it shapes and by which it is produced.[10] It seems a rather backhanded compliment to Kristeva when the editors of a volume on intertextuality defend her against her critics with the assertion that "the importance of Kristeva's work is not so much her reading of particular poets, or even of particular poetic genealogies, as her formulation of a theory of the subject and of language."[11] Where would the "formulation of a theory of the subject and of language" have its basis if not in a praxis of reading, of particular readings of particular subjects and of the modes in which they present themselves, and of particular formations of language?

But to pose the question in such a way might presuppose already too much; it might already fixate the relationship of theory and praxis in a simplistic linearity, harmony, and complementarity; it might posit even too much already by positing such terms as *theory* and *praxis* with their loaded ideological histories.

Given the conspicuous presence of the word *theory* in literary criticism, however, it cannot simply be disregarded. If, as Freud has observed, theorizing and speculation are always very close to phantasizing and prone to phantasmatic reifications, the opposition and resistance to theory in the name of pure untheoretical praxis is perhaps the most phantasmatic of all phantasies.

Walter Benjamin's essay "The Task of the Translator," which is at the center of the first essay and its 'echolalia' and is refracted and reflected throughout the other two essays, is a highly theoretical text. Yet one should not forget that it was written as Benjamin's preface to his translations of Baudelaire. The relationship between 'theoretical' pre-text and the praxis of translation is not clear at all. It was the difficulty of accounting in precise terms for the relationship between Benjamin's theory of translation (if it is one) and his praxis of translation that suggested the possibility of a gap and demanded attention. There is no metatheory of the relationship between theory and praxis, just as there is no metatheory of the relationship between what Benjamin calls "pure Language" and languages. Between them is a gap, a space of presentation, of *Darstellung:* a theater rather than a theory.

Pure Language is not an abstraction, not a concept, but the most concrete Here and Now of an intersection between texts and between languages. It is perhaps an idea, a constellation of the historically determined echoes between the texts in the resonance of a singular reading with all its accidents and coincidences.

What Benjamin calls pure Language seems to come close to what Derrida calls the "general text."[12] Both terms attempt to break out of the simple dichotomy of an immanence and interiority of language/text versus an outside reality that haunts many theories of realism and of language. Both Benjamin and Derrida aim at an articulation of intersections that cannot be thought of in terms of a dialectical sublation. Just as for Derrida there is no *hors-texte,* nothing outside the text,[13] for Benjamin there is nothing outside language: "The existence of language extends not only across all realms of human spiritual expression, which in some sense is always inhabited by language, but it extends principally onto everything."[14] These statements are a dangerous trap for quick readers, whether they embrace enthusiastically the notion that "everything is text and language" or whether they use such phrases as weapons in the battle against ivory-tower intellectuals and literary critics in the name of realism, social and political responsibility, and human interest. But as Rodolphe Gasché has pointed out, Derrida's formulation does not necessarily imply "that everything is text";[15] and Benjamin's formulation does not say that everything is language but that language extends onto everything ("erstreckt sich auf schlechthin alles"). In the same essay, Benjamin warns against "the view that the intelligible essence of a thing consists in its language— this view understood as a hypothesis is the great abyss to which all language theory threatens to fall prey, and to preserve itself above it, hovering above it, is its task."[16] Benjamin's insistence on a position *über* (over, above) the abyss designates, as a position over the abyss, not a panoptic overview but rather the *über* of *Übersetzung* and *Übertragung* (translation, transport, transfer), which, as the translations of Eros will show, is also the position of Eros. Eros is the one who, in Hölderlin's translation, above all *übernachtet;* he spans the night as the quintessential time-space of a "between" without limits. All delimitations emerge from it.

At the beginning and at the end is the impossibility of formulating a metatheory of pure Language. A gap opens up between Language and languages, between a theory of translation and its praxis, which shapes the praxis of reading in the following essays. They are essays in the literal sense: experiments of *Darstellung,* of presenting something that escapes representation.

A praxis of reading that emerges not from a rejection of theory, not from the phantasm of an innocence free of theory, but from the impossibility of theory in the kernel of theory will necessarily affect its object. Therefore, our praxis is not only a reading of texts but a reading *between* texts.

What does it mean to read between the texts? In a certain sense we always read, when we read, "between" (the lines, for example), because reading always involves a space of presentation where the figures gesture to each other in configurations and constellations that present more than any single figure means. But the structure of the space between the figures, which is determined by them and determines them, is shaped in more particular ways than by the mere universal differential relation of all signs.

The drama as a genre and theatrical presentation of interacting figures is particularly appropriate to demonstrate the changing structures of what constitutes 'between' and 'inter'. Thus one might differentiate a classical type of drama from a modern type on the basis of a radically different structure of the interspace they project on the stage.[17] Peter Szondi defines classical drama in terms of a dialogical dialectics of intersubjectivity.[18] Everything is rigorously enclosed in this intersubjective space of dialogue, of the *zwischenmenschliche Beziehung,* where the subjects and their fates disclose themselves in decisive acts.

Brecht's epic theater also delineates the theatrical space as a sphere of interactions, of interrelations: a space "between." But it is less an intersubjective space than a space of interests and the interrelations of production and consumption. Thus in his theatrical adaptation of Gorki's "The Mother," Brecht shifts the dramatic accent from the intersubjective relation between mother and son to the *Dritte Sache,* the "third cause," that is, the political cause and matter of interests and forms of production. This is not simply a matter of "political" versus "psychological" content but of radically different structures that affect the spatial relation between stage and audience.

As Szondi has shown, the dialogical-dialectical drama depends on an absolutely closed space that is separated from the space of the audience and ideally does not communicate with the audience. The separation finds its spatial expression in the orchestra pit, the "abyss" in Benjamin's formulation, which separates actors and audience.[19] But it is precisely this separation of physical space that allows for the most intense communication between audience and stage in a metaphorical space in the form of identification and absorption.

The battle against identification and absorption, against *Einfühlung,* is one of the guiding principles of Brecht's theater. Alienation and defamiliarization shatter the metaphorical space and its illusion of self-contained immanence. The actors address the audience, present demonstratively the split between actor and role, give their speeches as quotations, and distance the dramatic present as epic past. The world of the stage is ruptured by documentary fragments of the 'real' world. The theater pieces are pieces (*Stücke*) in a literal sense: constructions and constellations built from heterogeneous elements. Benjamin understands the epic theater above all as a leveling of the "abyss" of the orchestra pit.[20] The removal of the distance between audience and stage does not do away with that distance but transforms it into a split *within* the immanence of the closed spaces. It splits the agents on the stage and viewers in the audience within themselves and opens up another structure of the 'between'. Instead of individual, indivisible agents and worlds, elements of highly divisible characters and different worlds interact. Totalities are broken into pieces, and the broken pieces enter into readable constellations.

There are other structures of the 'between'. There is the one that opens up, for example, in the Jewish joke of Katzmann in Paris, who wants to hide his Jewish name in a good French name, only to find himself more Jewish than ever as *chat l'homme* (= shalom). In the intersection of two languages, between the German signifier "Katzmann" (= cat-man) and its literal French translation, a third language suddenly appears in the Hebrew "*shalom.*" Daniel Sibony describes this structure of a space between the languages as a void: "The Other, the unconscious is here in this hollow, in this void around which several languages are circling."[21] Baudelaire's verses in "Le cygne" call to this void in the name of Ovid. But the Jewish joke also underlines another dimension: the revelation, the readability of the third language, the truth effect in the intersection of the two languages assumes its full significance in a specific constellation of historical experience and suffering.

Neither this void nor Brecht's space of *Inter-esse,* of interests and appetites, is available to any given language as much as it shapes every language. Only in the echoes between languages and texts might it resound here and there: in the echolalia between Hölderlin, Benjamin, and Baudelaire, in the echoes between antiquity and modernity, and more precisely in the hollows and void of the names of the gods, invoked by Hölderlin, diagnosed as a void by Baudelaire, and recalled once more by Nietzsche; they finally arrive in the translations of Eros from antiquity to modernity, from Sophocles to Hölderlin, from Baudelaire to Benjamin, in the passing of Antigone and in the passing of Baudelaire's *passante.* These are the texts around which the following essays circle.

To be more precise, they are not simply circling around these texts, they fracture them. Reading the unwritten text between the texts, listening to the echoes between the texts breaks up the integrity of the individual text and reassembles the shattered fragments in new constellations.

This form of reading resembles not only our Nietzschean epigraph but also the kind of translation that Benjamin invokes: "Just as fragments of a vessel, in order to be joined together, must follow each other in the smallest detail, but need not resemble one another, so instead of making itself similar to the meaning of the original, the translation must rather, lovingly and in detail, inform [*sich anbilden*] in its own language the mode of meaning of the original to make both recognizable as broken parts of a greater language, just as fragments are the broken part of a vessel."[22] Almost a century before Benjamin, Heinrich Heine, the poet who, like Baudelaire, stood at the threshold of modernity,[23] understood his own work in terms of a fragmentation that is reassembled elsewhere. Commenting on his narrative on a trip through the Harz Mountains (1826), he writes: "The 'Harzreise' is and remains a fragment, and the colorful threads that are so nicely woven into it in order to make a harmonious whole are suddenly cut off as if by the scissors of the Fates. Perhaps I will weave them into songs to come, and what is now left in paltry silence will then be uttered fully. In the end it doesn't matter when and where something is uttered, if it is only uttered at all. May the individual works remain fragments, if they only form a whole in their combination."[24] What intervenes here with the cutting scissors is not a sovereign ironic consciousness, hovering above its creations, undoing and reassembling them in infinite freedom, but the compelling power of something else, figured in the "Fates."

A reading that does not merely follow the "nicely woven" texture of the texts but instead takes into account the cuts, the loose and frazzled threads, will enter a space between the texts, where other texts and textures are woven in the intermingling of texts and languages. There we might begin to read that which has never been written.

Happy Babel. Happy babble? Not so fast. The difference between Babel and babble might be as wide as that between Roland Barthes's *Babel heureuse* and the *babil* that is outside pleasure and *jouissance*, a mere foam of language, a frigid text.[25] But they are also as close as their phonetic resonances. There are no guarantees of arrival in the passages from echo to echo, from text to text, from language to language.

The ideological petrifications of academic and public critical scenarios make it difficult to address the question of truth and language outside the dichotomies of rhetorical proclamations and moralistic resentments that dominate the institutions of literary criticism. Ever since Nietzsche's text "On Truth and Lie in the Extra-moral Sense"[26] became the focus of critical attention,[27] Nietzsche's provocative answer to the loaded question "What, then, is truth?" has stirred critical aggressions that testify to profound anxieties. Here is Nietzsche's own answer to his question: "A mobile army of metaphors, metonymies, anthropomorphisms, in short, a sum of human relations that were poetically and rhetorically intensified, translated, ornated and that, after long use, seem firm, canonical, and binding to a people: truths are illusions of which one has forgotten that they are illusions, metaphors that are worn out and have lost their sensual impact, coins that have lost their image and have become mere metal, useless as coins."[28] No wonder, then, that Nietzsche has been declared the gateway to postmodernism,[29] which shares with other "posts" the charge of linguistic and rhetorical reductionism. But these historical displacements of major texts of modernism to postmodernity (including Kafka, Brecht, Joyce, and many others) may indicate a refusal to read the texts of modernism at their most disquieting points.

Most disquieting for many literary critics is the confrontation with that which constitutes the subject of the discipline. The phantasmatic instrumentalization of language as a "mere" vehicle or "mere" formality produces as its complement the phantasm of "real presences" as the true and legitimate ground of literature. The less epistemological and analytical attention that this dichotomy can sustain, the more rhetorical and moral pathos it will invest in its proclamation. This moral pathos stops at nothing; it even calls upon the Holocaust as its instrument.[30] Hölderlin's and Benjamin's texts occupy a certain privileged place in the following essays because of the particular way in which they not only address but stage the truth effects of language.

One of the privileged terms in which the late eighteenth century tries to capture the truth effect of language is *life:* the living sense as opposed to the dead letter. But to attain this living sense might require a deadly exposure. "Life in poetry now occupies most my thoughts and senses. I feel deeply how far away I still am from the goal of hitting it," Hölderlin writes in November 1798 to his friend Neuffer.[31] *Treffen*—to hit something, to hit the mark—is the word that marks for Hölderlin the lucky and dangerous moment of a constitutive impact. It is a lucky moment because it is the moment of the right constellation; it is dangerous because *treffen* is always also *getroffen sein:* to be hit, to have received the impact. The poet who wants to hit the mark must be hit by Apollo.[32] One of the Homeric epithets for Apollo is *hekatèbolos* (the one who hits everything from afar, the one who does not miss).[33] Pindar refers to the words of his poetry as arrows that will hit their target.[34] The opposite term in Greek is *hamartia:* the fault that misses the mark and characterizes the tragic hero. For Hölderlin, it is the *Treffen,* not the missing, which accounts for the tragic constellation: the tragic constellation is the constellation of genuine *Darstellung.*

As the moment of an impact, *Treffen* erases the difference between active and passive, between hitting and being hit. If *treffen* is the precondition for life in poetry, the impact also threatens the life that sustains the poetic word: in order to protect his "truest life," the poet shrinks from the "vulgarity of real life" (StA 6:289). But nobility depends on the vulgar; without it there is no poetic word. It must be colored by the "color of fate" [*die Farbe des Schiksaals*] (StA 6:290) as soon as it is expressed and presented. Yet in the passage quoted above from Heine, the scissors of the Fates cut the "colorful threads." Hölderlin's much derided literal translation of the Greek *kalchainein* in *Antigone* (v. 20) as "red coloring" ("Du scheinst ein rotes Wort zu färben") gives the testimony of truth to Antigone's word.

The word is true only insofar as it is colored and contaminated in the materialization of its appearance. Hölderlin translates the Greek *dèlois* as *Du scheinst* ("you seem to color a red word"); the Greek word can also mean "to reveal, to manifest." But the revelation, like the procreation by the father, is always uncertain. Only in the figural move from *zeugen* as procreation to *zeugen* as giving testimony, witnessing, can the word have a claim as living word. The transport from *zeugen* to "*zeugen*" is effected by a rupture, by the caesura that Hölderlin locates in the appearance of Tiresias in both *Oedipus* and *Antigone*. In *Oedipus*, Tiresias enters as the one who refuses to speak. Oedipus therefore calls him pitiless, or, literally, "hard, unsoftened" (*ategktos*), which Hölderlin translates as *farblos* (colorless, v. 340). He is outside the coloring of fate and *Darstellung;* he is the figure of the inexpressive that cuts, as the caesura, into the stream of expression and brings it to its truth. The 'living' word is the interrupted word as witness rather than a 'creative' procreation. Hölderlin's *Oedipus* translation marks this interruption most radically at a point when the Greek *ektribèsetai* (is annihilated) is given as *gezeugt seyn* (is procreated, v. 435).

Modern poetics cannot regress to the poetic ground or to the "living sense" in a simple and straight movement. It can only loosen up or, more violently, shake and rattle the firm forms of the given, as Hölderlin did, when he subjected German syntax to the violence of Pindar's Greek syntax. By translating Pindar's odes literally word for word, Hölderlin turns Pindar's *epeôn thesin* (the setting of the words) into a *Darstellung* that is a radical *Entstellung* (displacement) of German syntax and word order.

At one point of the poem *Brod und Wein,* Hölderlin stages the *treffend Wort,* the precise word, the word that hits the mark, in a pun between Greek and German:

Wo, wo leuchten sie denn, die fernhintreffenden Sprüche?
Delphi schlummert und wo tönet das große Geschik?
Wo ist das schnelle? wo brichts, allgegenwärtigen Glüks voll

Donnernd aus heiterer Luft über die Augen herein?
Vater Aether! so riefs und flog von Zunge zu Zunge
Tausendfach, es ertrug keiner das Leben allein;
Ausgetheilet erfreut solch Gut und getauschet, mit Fremden,
Wirds ein Jubel, es wächst schlafend des Wortes Gewalt
Vater! heiter! und hallt, so weit es gehet, das uralt
Zeichen, von Eltern geerbt, treffend und schaffend hinab

[Where, where do they still shine, the sayings that hit far into the distance? Delphi slumbers and where does the great fate still resound? Where is the quick one? Where does it irrupt over the eyes full of omnipresent bliss, thundering out of the serene air? Father Aether, thus it called and flew from tongue to tongue, thousandfold, no one supported life alone; distributed, such good gives joy and shared, with foreigners, it becomes jubilation; sleeping, the power (violence) of the word grows. Father! serene! and it resounds downward, hitting and creating, as far as it goes, the ageold sign, inherited from parents]. (vv. 61–70)

The resounding echo between "Vater Aether" and "Vater! heiter!" plays on the phonetic and semantic proximity of the Greek *(h)aitèr* (ether; clear, serene air) and the German *heiter* (serene). It also invokes the German idiom for a sudden, unforeseen event, coming *aus heiterer Luft* (out of the blue).

The precision of the word that hits the mark (of truth), its *Treffen,* is a matter of unforeseen suddenness; it "breaks in," it irrupts over the eyes like a lightning bolt, and its echo resounds like thunder.

The echo of this lightning and thunder opens up the theoretical reflections in section N of Benjamin's notes on the Parisian arcades: "In den Gebieten, mit denen wir es zu tun haben, gibt es Erkenntnis nur blitzhaft. Der Text ist der langnachrollende Donner" [In the areas with which we are dealing here, insight occurs only like a lightning bolt. The text is the thunder that resounds long after] (5:570). The lightning bolt also figures the structure of what Benjamin calls the dialectical image as a specific moment of historical readability in the constellation of past and present moments: "It is not the case that things past [*das Vergangene*] shed their light on present things [*das Gegenwärtige*], nor that present things shed their light on things past; but the image is that moment where the past enters like a lightning bolt into a constellation with the now. In other words: Image is dialectics in a standstill."[35] Benjamin differentiates *das Vergangene* (what is past, what has vanished) from *Vergangenheit* (the past as a more or less homogeneous and totalizable entity), and *das Gegenwärtige* (what is present) from *Gegenwart* (the present as homogeneous and totalizable entity). History is thus a constellation not of past and present but of past and present moments. There is no past that can be reconstructed; what is past has vanished. The dialectical image as the constellation of a specific past moment with a specific present moment is a *construction* where something becomes readable, where an insight, a recognition takes place. The melancholy ground of that recognition is the irrecoverable pastness of things past.

We recall this well-known passage from Benjamin in order to read it again in the constellation of some of the other texts that form and inform the following essays. At the same time it functions as a commentary on the structure of the echolalia produced in the confrontation of textual fragments. Two points must be emphasized: just as for Benjamin the historical constellation is a relationship not between two integral entities of time (past and present) but between fragmentary elements that have been blasted out of their context, the echoes here are produced between textual fragments. This raises another problem: What guarantees that such a constellation is more than pure subjective arbitrariness or witty wordplay at best? What guarantees any kind of objective insight and readability?

A sentence written a few pages earlier seems to offer little hope: there are no guarantees of arrival in the passages from echo to echo, from text to text, or from language to language. And yet there seems to be an insistence, shared by some of the most radical writers, that in and through the destructive, dissecting work of the text something 'true' must appear.

Hölderlin's poetry has articulated this postulate most directly in the poem *Germania:* "Muß zwischen Tag und Nacht/Einsmals ein Wahres erscheinen. Dreifach umschreibe du es,/Doch ungesprochen auch, wie es da ist,/Unschuldige, muß es bleiben" [Once, with one mark, something true must appear between day and night. Threefold you must circumscribe it, but unspoken also, as it is there, O innocent one, it must remain] (vv. 92–96). These lines will be discussed in the second essay of this book. It will suffice here to point out two aspects: not truth, but something true, a true moment or element (*ein Wahres*) appears, and it appears in a time-space 'between'.

More precisely, its appearance is not a statement of fact but presented in the modality of necessity: it must appear. It must appear at a certain point, at a certain time, when certain conditions are fulfilled. But as the use of *certain* in such expressions indicates: nothing is a priori less certain than a 'certain point in time'. Its certainty is strictly a posteriori, *nachträglich, après coup.* Its necessity is not that of a natural law but of a rhetorical postulate that sustains the labor of the text.

The labor of the text, the working through of the writer in and through that labor, is a necessary but insufficient condition of the postulated 'must'. Hölderlin not only writes about this labor and its necessity, but he stages it syntactically and rhetorically in a fragmentary essay. Its vertiginous unending periods of hypotaxis and parataxis perform what the essay calls the repetition "of the inner reflections and striving" that tears apart "the unreflected pure sensation" in the hope that it will emerge as an echo (*Widerklang*) and like a magical lightning bolt (*mit einem Zauberschlage*).[36] The *Zauberschlag* (magical bolt), like the *Blitzschlag* (lightning bolt), is prepared through the tortuous labor of working through, but its event cannot be guaranteed.

In theory at least, Brecht seems to be more optimistic. Like Benjamin's dialectical image, Brecht's theater pieces are an attempt at a dialectics at a standstill: a caesura intervenes in the continuities of story lines, freezes the gestures and movements at strategic points in order to reveal what Brecht calls *Gestus,* the underlying social and linguistic structures that shape individual gestures not so much as individual expressions but as expressions of social and historical conventions.

Brecht illustrates what he calls "gestural language" in a sentence from Luther's Bible translation. The biblical command "Tear out the eye that scandalizes you" (Matt. 5:30) is presented by Luther with a gestural caesura: "Wenn dich dein Auge ärgert: reiß es aus" [If your eye scandalizes you: tear it out].[37] Violence ties seeing and blinding together at the core of the gestural theater that, for Brecht, is based on a desire to see. But because the evidence of the eyes is insufficient, epic theater wants to be more than spectacle, and the eyes are subjected to violence. Not only are the images torn to pieces, interjected with heterogeneous material, but the eyes themselves might be torn out. Brecht's favorite term for the political function of his theater is *Eingriff,* a word with strong surgical connotations: active, surgical intervention into the body politic and into the social body.

The operation, the tearing apart of familiar contexts, serves the defamiliarization of the familiar. Brecht would like to keep a certain restraint on this operation; he distances himself from radical deformations. For the sake of a classical ideal and political control, he wants to draw the line against the radical defamiliarizations of modernity: "Dadaism and surrealism," he writes, "use defamiliarization effects of the most extreme kind. Their objects do not return from the estrangement. The classical defamiliarization, however, heightens understanding."[38]

Surrealism is the modern medium through which the limits of Brecht's and Benjamin's far-reaching affinity are drawn. Where Benjamin sees a specifically political image-space (*Bildraum*) and body-space (*Leibraum*), a kind of Dionysian theater of modernity where no limb of the familiar body remains untorn, Brecht sees the horrific image of a curious disfiguration of the hand: "[The surrealists] try to shock the observer, by interrupting, disappointing, displacing his associations when, for example, a woman has eyes instead of fingers on her hand."[39] The casualness of the example is the staging of an overdetermined constellation. Hand and eye are condensed in a monstrous organ of perception which displaces all relations of theory and praxis, of *vita activa* and *vita contemplativa.*

It would be a mistake, however, simply to oppose Brecht's distancing from the radical defamiliarizations and displacements of surrealism to Benjamin's valorization of the movement as an explosive political force.[40] Brecht's destructive energy is too strong to contain him in his own classical gesture, and Benjamin's "profane illumination" is too sober to be contained in the enthusiasm of dreams, no matter how radical their displacements might seem. The political and cultural critique of both Brecht and Benjamin articulates a threshold that displaces and reassesses familiar rhetorical oppositions, among them the one that was to become the politically most powerful one in the thirties, when, in the so-called expressionism debate, an irrational—and therefore potentially fascist—modernity was opposed to a rational, humanistic, and realistic art. As outdated as these oppositions might seem today in the light of a modernism that has long been canonized, their terms nevertheless continue to haunt the rhetorical battlefields of today's theoretical debates about modernism and postmodernism.

Benjamin's essay on surrealism begins with the simile of a power plant and the cognitive energy gained by a difference, the potential gradient that drives the power plant, in this case the difference and gradient between the German and French perspective on surrealism. The source of energy is a *Gefälle* (fall, gradient) and its first goal an explosive destruction that brings to a fall the given constructions. Just as Brecht's plays and their political energy are driven by all-consuming appetites, Benjamin's cognitive energy begins with destructions, explosions, and also consumptions. The figures of cannibalism and devouring have a conspicuous place in his work. Truly "a mobile army of metaphors, metonymies, anthropomorphisms" is at work here, but according to Nietzsche one that is set into motion against the illusions of truth that this army has set up in the first place.

The strategy is a precarious one. Its figures are full of tricks and traps. What guarantees that the lightning bolt that suddenly illuminates a figurative constellation of decontextualized, blasted elements is indeed the sober reading of a "profane illumination," rather than the result of the dreams and enthusiasms of religious and profane opiates? Like Baudelaire, who opposes the illusionary effects of hashish to the artistic illuminations, Benjamin confronts his "profane illumination of a materialist, anthropological inspiration"[41] with the effects of opium and hashish. But as Baudelaire's text constantly blurs the borderlines,[42] Benjamin delineates a threshold where drugs and dreams are not simply opposed to profane illumination; they are even seen as a precondition of sober illumination, a kind of pretraining and propaedeutics, albeit a dangerous one, which easily slips into an obscurantism, to which the surrealists were not always immune.

No text is immune, but no text that aims at moments of truth can avoid taking risks: the risk of dreaming, the risk of the figures and images, the risk of language and its play. Benjamin, like Breton, thus gives the right of way to image and language ("I will pass through where nobody yet has passed, hush!—After you, dearest language").[43] And yet he insists on the rigorous work of thought. He even concedes to the opium of religion a certain advantage over the profane because it is more rigorous.[44]

In the turns and leaps of Benjamin's work there is a consistent return to the problem of the constellation and figure as a moment of a true reading. The articulation of the problem can be located somewhat schematically at three major points of crystallization: the difference of *Sachgehalt* (factual content) and *Wahrheitsgehalt* (truth content) in the essay on Goethe's *Wahlverwandtschaften* and in the book on the German baroque *Trauerspiel;* the figure of the constellation in the preface of the *Trauerspiel* book; and, finally, in the relationship of dialectical image and dream in the later work. A closer look at these texts reveals a remarkably consistent pattern and structure.

The figure of the constellation is introduced as a figure of difference between 'idea' and 'phenomenon'. The idea does not incorporate the phenomena; it belongs to a "principally different sphere."[45] "Ideas are related to things as the constellations of the stars to the stars. That is to say: they are neither their concepts nor their laws."[46] This difference corresponds to the difference be-tween *Sachgehalt* and *Wahrheitsgehalt*. Between these two spheres there is *Darstellung:* the presentation of truth. *Darstellung* is first the dismemberment and dissection of the phenomena. Benjamin presents this dissection in two forms: in a philosophical form as the analytical dissection of things in concepts; and in a figurative form in the broken pieces that constitute the mosaic. Benjamin associates the "majesty of the mosaic with the powerful impact of a sacred image."[47] The mosaic as the figure of the idea, of the sphere of truth, and even of the sacred is composed of disparate pieces and has no direct relationship with the original things from which the pieces of the mosaic are broken off. And yet both the mosaic and the idea claim to be objective interpretations of the phenomenal world whose broken pieces constitute the image of the mosaic. There is, then, a certain paradox in philosophical (and critical) *Darstellung,* in the presentation of the true: the true never follows immediately and directly from the phenomena, the things, the factual subject matter (the *Sache*), and yet its *Darstellung* requires a rigorous working through the phenomena, a kind of in-sistent analysis, dissection, an insistent return to the same thing over and over, chipping off, as it were, piece by piece. But the re-arrangement of these pieces seems to require a leap, a lucky mo-ment, an objective historical and memorial time element that is not in anyone's control.

The leap from *Sachgehalt* to *Wahrheitsgehalt* is condensed in Benjamin's use of the German word *(Ur-)Sprung*. A *Sprung* is both a leap and a crack (in a glass, for example). It signals the rupture and suddenness in the transition from empirical phenomena to their (re-)presentation in the sphere of language, thus of their sig-nificance. As Hölderlin's echo of the original experience occurs *mit einem Zauberschlage* (with a magic bolt) after its painful disrup-tions in the seemingly futile repetitive back-and-forth of reflection, thus for Benjamin the criterion of the true leaps out of the com-mentary of the *Sachgehalt:* "mit einem Schlag entspringt."[48]

This suddenness of the leap is figured in Benjamin's later work in the lightning bolt of the dialectical image. The occurrence of the dialectical image is not a mystical intuition but the result—although uncontrollable—of a rigorous working-through of the phenomenal historical world and of a strategic interruption. These conditions differentiate the dialectical image both from the dream image and from the archaic image of the Jungian archetype. With the construction of the dialectical image, Benjamin moves closest to Freud both in the method of reading and in the construction of the readable. The dialectical image is not the dream but the interpretation of the dream in a moment of awakening.[49] It is therefore not simply an image but has its place in language.[50] The dream interpretation radically dissects the dream images and stories into their smallest elements and lets them enter through free association into constellations with other material of memory and daily life. Out of these constellations emerges the construction of another story: the reading of the dream, the reading of a desire and of the structures that organize the economy of desire.

Yet to say that the construction "emerges" is something of a contradiction: it denies the active 'constructive' element. The construction does not simply "emerge," but it is also not simply the result of a purposefully carried out intention. What Freud calls the "construction in analysis," what Benjamin thinks in the figure of the dialectical image, what Hölderlin points at in his "hint concerning presentation [*Darstellung*] and language" as the moment when, with one magical bolt, the echo and resonance of the original sensation and experience leap forth are all attempts to articulate a moment and place outside the dichotomy of pure intuition or inspiration and purposeful, controlled intentional thought. The latter became in the eighteenth century the enemy figure of true 'creative' production. "Es ist alles nur gedacht" [It is all only thought], Goethe wrote in July 1771 self-critically to Herder about his just-finished first version of *Götz von Berlichingen*—and through careful stylistic reworkings he produced a second version that gave the appearance of pure, unmediated expressiveness.

This paradoxical process from a first, relatively uninhibited draft, which is yet "nur gedacht," to a final version that gives the illusion of pure unmediated expression through elaborate stylistic revisions can be taken as a paradigm for the underlying dominant aesthetic principles of the late eighteenth century and the nineteenth: its axiom is to hide the construction, to hide the artifice and to give the illusion of nature.

If in contrast there is a common principle in modernist aesthetics, it might be called a poetics of the caesura: the interruption of the aesthetic illusion, the laying bare of the artifice, the 'poeticity' of the work. The aesthetics of illusion is essentially a bourgeois aesthetics, parallel to an economic market theory that covers the violence of the market competition and exploitation of labor with the veil of a naturally regulated economy of supply and demand. If the bourgeois aesthetics aims at a lullaby to sleep and dream, the poetics of the caesura is the alarm clock that mercilessly interrupts the dream and lays bare the stuff that dreams are made of.

But as surrealism, among other modernist movements, indicates, the relationship of the attitude of the artist as engineer or constructivist and the dreamer is not that simple. The glass and steel architectures of modernity are no less immune to dreams and phantasmagorias than the elaborate constructions of a baroque allegory. Both have in common the paradoxical side-by-side and interlacing of rational construction and phantasmagoric quality.

Kafka, who pointed out the "dreamlike" quality of his work, was also one of the most lucid and inexorable readers of these dreams. In his readings, construction assumes a highly ambivalent position: "Mich ergreift das Lesen des Tagebuchs. Ist der Grund dessen, daß ich in der Gegenwart jetzt nicht die geringste Sicherheit mehr habe. *Alles erscheint mir als Konstruktion*" [I am touched (seized) reading the diary. Is the cause of it, that in the present time I have no longer the slightest security (certainty). *Everything appears to me as a construction*], Kafka writes on November 19, 1913, in his diary.[51] Even the syntax testifies to the utter insecurity and uncertainty: "Ist der Grund dessen . . ." has the syntactical structure of a question, but the period at the end give it the character of an assertion.

The site of construction is also the site of allegory, which asserts itself in the poetry of Heine and Baudelaire as much as in the critical writings of Benjamin and Paul de Man. It asserts itself in that split where Kafka's writing chases after itself: "Ich bin wirklich wie ein verlorenes Schaf in der Nacht im Gebirge" [I am really like a lost sheep in the night in the mountains]. But even this allegorical lost sheep in the mountains at night is perhaps too large a claim, and thus Kafka adds another turn of the screw: "oder wie ein Schaf, das diesem Schaf nachläuft" [or like a sheep that runs after that (lost) sheep].

What is lost is irrevocably lost. The allegorical construction does not recover the lost sheep, but it illuminates the status of the I whose being is produced in the running after itself, after its elfish being.

Between sheep and lost sheep, between an analyst and a lost analysant, between a text and a lost reader, and always between themselves, dialectical images and constructions may precariously take shape. Very precariously: "so wie z. B. die Kante eines großen Gebäudes im Nebel erscheint und gleich verschwindet" [just as for example the edge of a building appears in the fog and vanishes immediately].[52] An insight in the blindness that immediately vanishes in the blindness it produces. In the blinking of the eye where the translations of Eros have their blinding site, in the moment, in the *Augenblick* of a passing: Antigone, for example, *une passante* in mourning. A lightning bolt, then darkness.

And yet there remains an insistence from Hölderlin to Kafka, Benjamin, and Freud that something true occurs. For Freud, for example, there is a difference between yes and no, even if the no might be an emphatic yes. This difference, which Freud attempts to articulate in one of his late essays, is not in the stability of yes or no but in a precarious construction somewhere between them.[53]

The following three essays are an exercise in such constructions. There is no a priori guarantee of the outcome of the experiment of a *Darstellung* through intertextual echoes. Only *nachträglich*, after the fact, will the construction of the reading prove or disprove itself.

1. Echolalia

echolalia [Gr. *echo*, an echo, and *lalia*, from *lalein*, to babble] a form of mental disorder in which the patient automatically repeats words heard by or addressed to him.—*Webster's Third New International Dictionary*

Mais ce ressassement sans terme de mots sans contenu, cette continuité de la parole à travers un immense saccage de mots, telle est justement la nature profonde du silence qui parle jusque dans le mutisme, qui est parole vide de paroles, écho toujours parlant au milieu du silence.—Maurice Blanchot

An abyss seems to open up between the *écho toujours parlant au milieu du silence,* that echo that Blanchot hears speaking in the middle of silence, and the babble of automatic repetition in the clinical definition of the word. The criteria of authenticity, truth, and the fullness of the word seem to be at stake in the space between the empty word (*la parole vide*) and the word without words (*parole vide de paroles*) that keeps speaking in silence.

According to Blanchot it is an *echo* that speaks. And it is an echo that Benjamin locates in that space of transition from language to language in translation: "It is the task of the translator to find that intentionality toward the language into which he translates, from which the echo of the original is evoked in it. . . . Translation, however, does not find itself, as poetry does, in the interior of the mountain forest of language itself, but outside of it, opposite to it, and without entering into it, it calls in the original, calls it in at that unique place where the echo in one's own language is capable to render the resonance of the work of a foreign language."[1] Benjamin's syntax itself produces at this point the density of a mountain forest. What is called and what resonates poses some problems to the reading and translation of this passage, specifically at that unique place where, according to Benjamin, the echo is produced and where Benjamin enacts it in the echo of a double *hinein* . . . *hinein,* which, if one listens with an open ear for the phonetic resonances, can be heard not only as "into" but also as *hin-ein* (gone the one), or *hi-nein* (here no). Benjamin writes that translation calls or shouts the original into the mountain forest, where it might, however, already be if it is poetry, and if poetry is, in contrast to translation, already in the interior of the mountain forest of language. Harry Zohn's English translation simply makes the original, which is called or shouted into the forest, disappear: "[Translation] calls into [the forest] without entering."[2] In another translation, the places are reversed: "and, without entering, it calls into the original, into that single place . . . ," writes one of Benjamin's most subtle readers.[3]

It seems that the access to this unique place where the echo or its effects take place can be reached only through detours. We might begin by noticing how the word "echo" emerges here and there in rather different texts. Thus Paul de Man hears certain echoes in Benjamin's essay: ". . . a figure of the poet as an almost sacred figure, as a figure which echoes sacred language. . . . But this tone hangs over the German academic discourse and over a certain concept of poetry which were then current. There are many echoes of it in the way Benjamin approaches the problem, at least superficially seen. . . . It is not just in the form of echoes that this is present in Benjamin, it almost seems to have been part of the statement itself."[4] The echo appears once more in the discussion following the lecture: "But the theme of the Frankfurt School interpretation of Benjamin is shot through with messianic elements which certainly are there, as a desire in Benjamin, but which Benjamin managed to control by an extraordinarily refined and deliberate strategy of both echoing themes, allowing them to enter his text, but then displacing them in his text in such a way that an attentive reading would reveal them."[5] Echo here refers to the sacred and messianic sphere. It appears first as the echo of a certain tone of the sacred in the academic discourse of Benjamin's time, which resonates in Benjamin's text. But de Man goes a step further when he states that it "is not just in the form of echoes that this is present in Benjamin, it almost seems to have been part of the statement itself." The sacred seems to enter into the tone itself, not just its echo. Echo and original tone no longer seem clearly separated. There is indeed a strong tendency in the Benjamin literature to read the sacred and messianic moments as the substance of his texts, as if the messianic and the sacred could be present in the content of the text. According to these readings, the sacred and the messianic would function as a ground and guarantee for the fullness of the word. Against such readings, de Man invokes Benjamin's texts as an echo, as a deliberate strategy of echoing themes that allows at the same time a displacement of the original tones. To be sure, there is, besides the echo, also something of the original tone of the sacred in Benjamin's tone, "as a desire in Benjamin," but the echo allows a corrective displacement of the desire. This displacement enters into a complex constellation with that other "unique place where the echo in one's own language is capable to render the resonance of the work of a foreign language." It is the task of the translator to find that unique strategic place where the echo can be produced, in order to make audible and perceptible in the resonance that pure language that is intended by all languages. And it would be the task of the critic to reveal, in a strategic arrangement of echoes, the original tones as elements of a wishful thinking. De Man uses the not quite innocent word "reveal" in this context. The echo strategy makes possible a revelation of the wishful nature of 'revelation' in language: a revelation of revelation.

As in psychoanalysis, it is the task of rhetorical analysis to direct the attention to that which produces certain effects instead of being seduced by the effects. What is thus revealed to the attentive reader are certain messianic tones in Benjamin's text, but they are revealed as elements of a wishful thinking, of a desire. If they are confused with cognition and insight, they turn into phantasms.

Yet the status of what de Man calls a "desire in Benjamin" cannot be easily defined. De Man links it with a tonal dimension of the text. It is first a certain tone that hangs over the German academic discourse and resonates as echo in Benjamin's texts; later it is also the tone of this text itself which many critics confuse with that which Benjamin actually says: "this pathetic mixture of hope and catastrophe and apocalypse which Hartman captures, which is present certainly in Benjamin's tone, but not so much in what he says."[6]

This difference between "tone" and what Benjamin says takes a curious turn in the context of Benjamin's text. This text namely says also that what is said and meant is less important in translation than the "mode of saying and meaning" (*die Art des Meinens*). One form in which this mode of meaning presents itself is precisely the "tone": "Faithfulness to the individual word in translation almost never can render the full sense that it has in the original. This sense namely, in its poetic significance for the original, cannot be exhausted in what is meant, but gains its significance only in the way in which what is meant is tied to the mode of meaning in the specific word. One usually expresses this fact in the formula that words carry a tone of feeling [*Gefühlston*] with them."[7] Benjamin takes recourse to common usage in order to point out something that is constitutive for the opening of languages onto Language. And this something is not only, as one usually says, a tone of voice in which something more than the semantic content of words is communicated, but specifically a *Gefühlston*, a tone of feeling.[8] This notion of a *Gefühlston* not only opens up the doors to "pathos" in the widest sense of the word (including that "pathetic mixture of hope and catastrophe and apocalypse"), but it might even be considered the condition of that "intentionality toward Language" from which or out of which the echo seems to be produced ("It is the task of the translator to find that intentionality toward the language into which he translates, from which the echo of the original is evoked in it"). One might also argue that by establishing intentionality as a fundamental energizing principle of language, as an *energeia* that pushes toward something, desire is given a rather strong place in language. It might even occupy that unique "place where the echo in one's own language is capable to render the resonance of the work of a foreign language."

De Man's critical sobriety acknowledges the presence of a messianic tone in Benjamin's text—as a desire; but he neutralizes it, as it were, through a strategy of isolation, by separating the tone from what is said. In doing so he attributes a considerable force of control to the author: "a desire in Benjamin, but which Benjamin managed to control by an extraordinarily refined and deliberate strategy of both echoing themes." The invocation of the author's control might at the same time point at something that threatens authorial control.

Whatever it is that is invoked in the tone, it is something that seems constitutive of the relationship of a text to language and of languages to Language. At the same time, this tone as a *Gefühlston* seems to render more difficult the recognition of the relation to language—the text's 'linguisticity', its *Sprachlichkeit;* it might even block the recognition or veil it under the affective vibrations of the tone. Only through the displacing effect of an echo strategy might the constitutive linguistic relation be accessible.

When de Man speaks of *echo* and *echoing* in Benjamin, he uses the word, at least on one level, in the familiar sense of inter- and intratextual resonances and allusions.[9] Indeed, Benjamin's text is permeated by intertextual resonances. De Man hears both messianic and Nietzschean 'nihilistic' elements as the two "echoing themes" that control the text. The manifold echoes of early German romanticism have often been noticed.[10] The passage on the echo in the essay is itself an echo not only of the most famous poem of Baudelaire's *Fleurs du mal*—"Comme de longs écho qui de loin se confondent" ("Correspondances," v. 5)—but also of Hölderlin's poetry, which presents and understands itself as translation and echo:

> so kam
> Das Wort aus Osten zu uns,
> Und an Parnassos Felsen und am Kithäron hör' ich
> O Asia, das Echo von dir und es bricht sich
> Am Kapitol

[Thus came to us from the East the Word, and on the rocks of Parnassos and on Kithairon I hear, O Asia, the echo from you and it is refracted on the Capitol]. ("Am Quell der Donau," vv. 35–39)[11]

Hölderlin's poetic praxis and theory occupy a privileged place in this essay on the task of the translator, which is at the same time the preface to Benjamin's own translations from the *Fleurs du mal* and resonates with Baudelaire's language. Hölderlin's translation of the Sophoclean *Oedipus* and *Antigone* figure as the model of translation.[12] Even more than model, they are "Urbild zum Vorbild" [archetype of the model] (4:21); thus they approach the sacred text—but there are abysses: "In these translations meaning plunges from abyss to abyss until it threatens to get lost in bottomless depths of language."[13] Here one may hear the echo from Hölderlin's poem "Hyperions Schicksalslied":

Es schwinden, es fallen
Die leidenden Menschen
Blindlings von einer
Stunde zur andern,
Wie Wasser von Klippe
Zu Klippe geworfen
Jahr lang ins Ungewisse hinab

[Suffering humans vanish and fall, unseeing, from one hour to the next, like water, thrown from cliff to cliff yearlong down into uncertain depth]. (vv. 18–24)

In the echo resounds the unbridgeable difference between suffering humans and blissful gods, between the profane and the sacred.

The abyss of difference has its resonance and echo in Benjamin's book on the baroque *Trauerspiel,* specifically in the abyss constituted by allegory and its "contemplative calm with which it immerses itself into the abyss between pictorial being [*bildliches Sein*] and meaning,"[14] as well as in the abyss between writing and sound: "Writing and sound stand in a very tense polarity in opposition to each other. . . . The chasm between signifying written figure [*Schriftbild*] and intoxicating language sound, compels the gaze to look into the depth at the moment when the fixed massif of the meaning of the word is torn up."[15] The intoxicating sound of language is opposed to the signifying figures and lines of writing, its Apollonian image to the Dionysian drunken music of spellbinding sounds: between them, meaning is torn to pieces. The rupture opens an abyss in language—*Sprachtiefe:* a depth in and of language, a depth of something that is yet pure surface.

The rhetoric of the abyss carries a seductive pathos. It seems that Benjamin is well aware of it, when he insists already in the earlier essay "Über die Sprache überhaupt und über die Sprache des Menschen" ("On Language in General and on the Language of Man") that the most important thing is not to fall prey to the spell of the abyss, not to fall into it: "The view that the intelligible essence of a thing consists in its language—this view understood as a hypothesis is the great abyss to which all language theory threatens to fall prey, and to preserve itself above it, hovering above it, is its task."[16] The task of language theory and the task of the translator meet in the double demand: to tear open the meaning, to direct the gaze, in the most fleeting touch of meaning, toward the depth of language and yet not fall into the depth.

The Hölderlinian echo intones the threat of such a plunging into the bottomless, empty depth of language where meaning is liquidated in the intention toward Language and where thought is carried away by the torrents of this liquid language. But as echo it also preserves itself, hovering above it, allowing the determinate word to emerge from the liquid flow, through a sequence of refractions where the word is broken and reinvoked, fading in and fading out.

The fragmentary poem "Am Quell der Donau," in which Hölderlin invokes the word as an echo from Asia, has no beginning. It 'begins' on the lower part of a partially empty page with a tone, a "melodischen Strom, von der herrlichgestimmten, der Orgel" [a melodious flow from the magnificently tuned, from the organ].[17] But this tone stands under the rule of a *Wie* (as, like), as a simile that only points at the coming word: "so kam / Das Wort." And this word is *echo*.

The coming of the word is staged in a sequence of refractions, marked by the stations of occidental history, names of mountains and mountain forests, which accentuate moments and transitions of European linguistic and cultural history: the Greek mountains and mountain forests of Parnassus and Cithaeron, the hills of Rome, the Alps. Each refraction, each breaking of the word is another echo of an inaccessible origin which Hölderlin's occidental text calls with the Greek/Latin name *Asia*.

Hölderlin's invocation of *Asia* is itself the echo of a Greek echo. It recalls the Euripidean *Asiètan . . . achan* (Asian echo) in *Iphigenia in Tauris* (v. 180). In the dialogue between Iphigenia and the chorus, the chorus responds to Iphigenia's lamentation over her lost homeland with an "Asian barbaric countersong": "antipsalmous ôidas hymnôn t'/Asìetan soi barbaron achan/despoina g'exaudasô" [countersongs as a barbarian echo I will sing to you, mistress] (vv. 179–81). The Asian echo as a barbarian countersong to the Greek heroine's lamentation song corresponds to the preceding naming of the lost homeland not only as Argos and Greece but as Europe: "Hellados euippou pyrgous/kai teichè chortôn t'eudendrôn/exallaxas' Eurôpan/patrôôn oikôn hedras" [Palaces and cities of Greece, rich with horses, I have left and Europe full of meadows and trees, the place of my father's house] (vv. 133–36). In Hölderlin's countersong and echo, the Asian barbarian countersong returns as the archetypal tone of the European word. This explicit inversion in the echo points at an implicit inversion in the Greek text: the barbarian Asian countersong tells the story of the origin of Iphigenia.

Hölderlin's poetics is based on a theory of tones and alternation of tones. Such a grounding of poetry in the elusive dimension of tonality where any semantic determination is liquified threatens to plunge poetics into bottomless depths. Hölderlin counters the threat with a systematized theory of a calculable alternation of tones which he records in a series of permutation tables.[18] Hölderlin's poetics of "tones" points, like Benjamin, at a register of language that is 'meaningless', presemantic, even asemantic.[19] Ismene can therefore, in Hölderlin's translation, still 'hear' Antigone even in the moment of a radical nonunderstanding: "Sinnlos, doch lieb in liebem Tone sprichst du" [Senseless, but lovely, in a lovely tone you speak] (v. 101). She hears what Benjamin calls *Gefühlston,* a dimension that also in Hölderlin appears in words like *fühlen* (to feel, to sense) and *Fühlbarkeit* (the potential of something to be felt, its tangibility).

Feeling and *Fühlbarkeit* stand, like Benjamin's *Gefühlston,* in a specific relation to language. Benjamin's *Gefühlston* is defined as the relation of meaning to the mode of meaning, "the way in which what is meant is tied to the mode of meaning in the specific word." Hölderlin's *Fühlbarkeit* appears as receptivity for language through which a totality imparts itself. It is mediated and produced by a process of separations and reflections: "The tangibility [*Fühlbarkeit*] of the whole progresses in the same degree and relation in which the separation in the parts and the center, through which the parts and the whole are most tangible, progresses."[20] What emerges from this process is the echo of an origin in an anticipation of language: "Resonance [*Wiederklang*] of the original living sensation . . . , it is in this moment where one can say that language is anticipated [*geahndet wird*]."[21] This anticipation of language corresponds to a remembering in language: "Just as cognition anticipates language, language remembers cognition."[22] What Hölderlin calls "cognition" [*Erkenntnis*] spans the whole range from the "still unreflected, pure sensation of life" through the dissonances of reflection, striving, and imaginative thinking [*Dichten*] to "the resonance of original living sensation" as an echo produced in a "higher divine receptivity" from which that language emerges in which life imparts itself as remembrance and echo. Language is thus not an expression of cognition. Cognition aims at an anticipation or divination of a language *in* which it can impart itself as remembrance.

This figure of imparting and communication resounds not only in content but in the literal echoes of words through Benjamin's essay on the task of the translator. Hölderlin's formula appears in Benjamin's formulation as an anticipation [*Ahnung*] of pure Language: "and it is precisely this [pure Language] whose anticipation [*Ahnung*] and description is the only perfection that a philosopher can hope for, and it is intensively hidden in translation."[23] Benjamin continues and expands his reflections on the philosophy of language in the book on the baroque *Trauerspiel;* and here appears also the other side of anticipation: remembering in language. Hölderlin's first moment of cognition as the "original sensation of life" which language remembers after the dismemberment of reflection appears in Benjamin's text as an original or primal hearing (*Urvernehmen,* 1:216 ff.): it is the task of the philosopher, according to Benjamin, to reinstate the symbolic character of the word in its primacy in his presentation through a remembrance that first goes back to the primal hearing.

Benjamin contrasts this remembrance with any kind of revelatory discourse which is explicitly forbidden to philosophy. The original sensation that determines the tone of language in the primal hearing can only be remembered in the resonances of echoes.

Accordingly, any text that deals with this dimension of language and with what Benjamin calls "pure Language" cannot simply represent it (if it would do so, it would fall into the abyss of pseudorevelatory discourse); it has to find a mode of procedure where it can invoke the primal moment without reifying it.

In order to talk of the echoes and their effects, our own presentation has to enter in the indirect discourse of the echoing texts. This determines a form of presentation that attempts to listen to the intertextual echoes in the constellations of textual fragments. The procedure is dictated by the hypothesis that what Benjamin calls "pure Language" and which, by definition, cannot be expressed in any language (accordingly also not in the languages of Benjamin, Hölderlin, or Baudelaire) might perhaps become tangible and noticeable (*merkbar*) in the intertextual echo effects.

Benjamin's formulation marks the difference between a translation that is merely a *deaf equation* and the temporally delayed echo effect of true translation with the German word *merken* (notice, sense, perceive a mark): it is true translation's most proper quality (a quality and property that 'falls to it' [*zufällt*] as if by accident or chance [*Zufall*]) to take note [*auf . . . merken*] of the afterripening of the foreign word and of the pangs of one's own word.[24] The passage has gained a certain notoriety through de Man's translation and interpretation of the *Wehen* as "death pangs" instead of "birth pangs." Some Germanists seemed rather happy to have caught this intruder in their territory with a blatant philological error. De Man's translation indeed poses a riddle. He not only says that *Wehen* as the plural of *Weh* could have the connotation of all kinds of sufferings beyond the specific idiomatic use in which the plural generally does refer to birth pangs, but he calls it a "mystery" that both the English and French translators would translate it in the sense of "birth pangs."[25] A translator hardly seems to have another choice, given the idiomatic use as well as the context in Benjamin's essay that seems to posit a clear correlation between the dying of the word in the original and its birth in another. Benjamin's own translation of Baudelaire's line "les douleurs des femmes en gésine" in "Crépuscule du matin" (v. 18) as "Die Wehen Schwangerer" might offer further support for *Wehen* as "birth pangs."

De Man's intrusive interruption of the idiomatic usage deranges the natives' ease and coziness in their language precisely at the moment when the alienating effect of translation is at stake: "We think we are at ease in our own language, we feel a coziness, a familiarity, a shelter in the language we call our own, in which we think that we are not alienated. What the translation reveals is that this alienation is at its strongest in our relation to our own original language, that the original language within which we are engaged is disarticulated in a way which imposes upon us a particular alienation, a particular suffering."[26] The interruption and disturbance of the idiomatic familiarity of *Wehen* as "birth pangs" is performed not only through a superscription of the paradigmatic possibilities of *Wehen* over its idiomatic use but also through its inscription in Benjamin's text and its relation there to the word *Nachreife* (afterripening), which, in de Man's text, echoes with the sweet delicate decadence of a *Spätlese* wine (made of late, rotten grapes) and the literary melancholy of Stifter's *Nachsommer*. The intertextual echoes of the *nach* and *spät* enter into a constellation with the intratextual echo of the *Nachreife* with the *Nachleben* and *überleben* of the original in translation. What does it mean to survive in an afterlife? If the original lives on, after its death in the afterlife of translation, the translation confirms the death of the original; the birth pangs of its rebirth in the afterlife of translation might then very well be also its death pangs.

There is another echo in de Man's argument and in Benjamin's *merken* of the *Nachreife,* one either of them might or might not have heard. In his *Oedipus* translation Hölderlin translates the anaphorically repeated Greek *phthinousa* (vanishing) with the

German verb *merken*: "Sie merkt den Tod in Bechern der frucht-
barn Erd'/In Heerden und in ungeborener Geburt" [She notices
(senses, marks) death in the cups of fertile earth, in the herds and
in unborn birth] (FA 16:82–83, vv. 25–26). The marking spot is the
vanishing in and of that which is fertile and promises birth.

Merken is not a direct perception of an object but a reading of
traces. What is marked and can be remarked at the vanishing
spot is radically belated and deferred: *nachträglich*. What becomes
noticeable, perhaps even readable, in the belated effects of the
echoes between texts is independent of authorial intention. A
phrase, a word, a phoneme even, a mere tone may become the car-
rier of unforeseen transports. Thus Rimbaud's pale Ophelia ("ô
pâle Ophélie") appears like an echolalia in the "Opal des Him-
mels" (the opal of the sky) which sparkles over Brecht's drowned
girl.[27] Ophelia's pale corpse is transported from one linguistic shore
to another; and we do not know whether Brecht, if he knew the
French original at all, remembered the French paleness when his
vowel intoxication transformed it into the sparkling jewel in his
German palinode of Rimbaud's poem. Ophelia continues to float
through the streams and rivers of translations. Benjamin's translation seems to remember her dismembered name when he renders
Baudelaire's alliteration in "Le cygne" (v. 48): *orphelin . . . fleurs*
in the German alliteration of *Blumenhäuptern bleichen*. Thus
Baudelaire's orphaned Ophelia pales in the alliterative babbling of
the German florilegium of letters.

When the echo approaches echolalia, we enter that space of
translation where, according to Benjamin, "meaning plunges from
abyss to abyss until it threatens to get lost in bottomless depths of
language."

There is something baroque in a mode of reading which con-
structs its figures in the recombination of fragmented textual
pieces. Indeed, Benjamin pointed out precisely such procedures as
techniques of the baroque drama: "In anagrams, in onomatopoetic
turns, and in many other linguistic virtuoso acts, the word, the syl-
lable, and the sound swagger, emancipated from any connection
with meaning, as things that can be allegorically exploited. . . .

Thus language is broken to pieces in order to give it over in its fragments to a transformed and intensified expression. . . . The shattered language no longer serves mere communication in its pieces, and it establishes its dignity as a newborn object next to the gods, rivers, virtues, and similar forms of nature that oscillated into the allegorical."[28] In this transcendence of communication and meaning toward an intensified expression, the baroque procedure resembles the task that Benjamin ascribes to the translator: "Just as fragments of a vessel, in order to be joined together, must follow each other in the smallest detail, but need not resemble one another, so instead of making itself similar to the meaning of the original, the translation must rather, lovingly and in detail, inform [*sich anbilden*] in its own language the mode of meaning of the original to make both recognizable as broken parts of a greater language, just as fragments are the broken part of a vessel."[29] But whereas the baroque technique characterizes an allegorical procedure, the task of the translator seems to aim at the symbol.

The antithesis of symbol and allegory, of pure Language and the language of judgment, which the book on the baroque drama unfolds, is condensed in the antithesis of sound and meaning in an echolalia that is struck by meaning: "When the echo of all things, the proper domain of a free play of sound, is struck [*befallen*] as it were by meaning, it had to be the ultimate demonstration as a revelation of Language [*des Sprachlichen*] as that time felt it."[30] Benjamin reads in these echo plays "the stylistic law of bombast, the formula of 'Asian words.'"[31] Once more the Asian echo emerges unexpectedly from the rhetorical tradition as an anticlassical, 'barbarian' countersong, in which now a revelation of Language is demonstrated in the specific form as it was felt by the baroque period.

Language, pure Language, does not exist, cannot be grasped and perceived, but it 'is' there in the tangible effects between languages and in the crevices within languages (between sound and meaning, for example, as sound and fury, for example) where it can be 'felt', in what Benjamin calls the *Gefühlston,* the mode of meaning which is specific to every language and every time. Thus the abyss between sound and meaning is specifically the baroque *Gefühlston* and its stylistic bombast. When this bombast, this anti-classical *stylus Asiaticus,* transports the Asian echo into the eighteenth century, its effects emerge according to Benjamin (who follows A. W. Schlegel in this remark) no longer from sound and image but from word combinations and word positions. It is the pioneering eighteenth-century German poet Klopstock who reveals this transition. Klopstock was the only model for lyrical poetry, outside of antiquity, which Hölderlin acknowledged in his search for the modern echo from Asia. The Greek model for Hölderlin is Pindar, whose odes Hölderlin rendered in a word-for-word translation, which shattered all German syntax and word position in order to fray a path for Hölderlin's most 'proper' late diction.

In his translation of Pindar's third Olympian ode, Hölderlin translates the Greek "epeôn de thesin" [the position (arrangement) of words] as "der Worte Gestalt" [the form or shape of words—with the specific connotation of a whole, integral form]. But Hölderlin's word-for-word translation, the "literality in the translation of the syntax,"[32] which Benjamin demands of translation, liquidates precisely *der Worte Gestalt* in German, that is, the German syntax, its idiomatic integral forms. The syntactical form of the original displaces and disfigures the form of the language of translation and opens it up toward Language as an *arcade* in the syntactical "wall before Language" (4:18).

But it also is an opening toward the Babel in Baudelaire's *Rêve parisien,* the "Babel d'escaliers et d'arcades" ("Gestuftes Babel von Arkaden" in Benjamin's translation), the Babel of stairs and arcades in a sphere where the organic and liquid world of plants and rivers is petrified and crystallized. Instead of the water "von Klippe/Zu Klippe geworfen" [thrown from cliff to cliff] whose echo tears open the "bottomless depths of language" in Benjamin's essay, everything in this poem is in dreamlike petrification, and the arcade in the wall only opens to other walls ("A des murailles de métal" [v. 20]). The ultimate, unheard-of terror is the absolute absence of tones in this dream world: "Tout pour l'oeil, rien pour les oreilles / Un silence d'éternité" [Everything for the eye, nothing for the ears / a silence of eternity] (v. 52–53), which, however, begins to resound in the poetic echoing tonality of *oeil—rien—oreilles*—an echo *toujours parlant au milieu du silence*.

The word as arcade in the wall of syntax not only breaks a passage through the syntax but forms a vertical line, mounting and descending like a staircase, in relation to the horizontal linearity of syntax. The steps of this stair conform to the levels and steps of meaning in traditional allegory as well as to the descending steps of intention (*absteigenden Intentionsstufen*) of melancholy in Benjamin's book on the baroque drama (1:334). A step in German is also an *Absatz* (something set off, a paragraph, an off-sentence, the breaking up of the sentence). In the breaks produced by the steps interrupting the syntax, the momentary hold of a precariously fixed meaning intersects with the unrestrained plunge of liquified meaning from step to step, from cliff to cliff into the bottomless depths of Language. Both in his book on the baroque drama and in the essay on the task of the translator Benjamin affirms that there is a stop, a hold.

But in both cases there is no holding on to meaning. To the contrary, it is a radical liquidation of meaning. Benjamin posits a hold where "meaning has ceased to be the watershed of streaming revelation."[33] It might be no more than the echo of a sound, just as in Hölderlin's poem "Brod und Wein" the power and violence of the word (*des Wortes Gewalt*), even the most ethereal word, grows like the word *Äther* (ether) in the returning echo sound *heiter* (serene): "und hallt, so weit es geht, das uralt / Zeichen, von Eltern geerbt, treffend und schaffend hinab" [and it resounds, as far as it goes, the age-old sign, inherited from parents, downward it sounds hitting the mark and creative] (vv. 65–70). And Walter Benjamin, listening to a language thus expanded and permeated by power ("einer so erweiterten und durchwalteten Sprache" [4:21]), perceives a hold in it, one that is given ("es gibt ein Halten"): a gift (*Gabe*) and a task (*Aufgabe*) for the translator. Already the Greeks heard in the word *ècho* the word *echein* (to hold).

Echo, reflection, refraction, rupture, steps are the returning figures of pure Language. Thus the "descending steps of intentionality" in melancholy find their corresponding complement in the mirroring of mounting steps: "Faithfulness is the rhythm of the emanating descending steps of intentionality in which the mounting steps of neoplatonic theosophy are mirrored transformed and full of correspondences."[34] In the figure of the mounting and descending steps Language appears as a rhythmic intermittence. Faithfulness to this Language, then, is guaranteed not in semantics and fixed meanings but in rhythm and correspondences.

Benjamin did not translate Baudelaire's "Correspondances." But the echoes from this poem produce the virtual space of the presentation of Benjamin's philosophy of translation. It is a linguistic space where identity and nonidentity, symbol and allegory intermingle "comme de longs échos qui de loin se confondent" [like long echoes that from afar melt together]. Baudelaire's poem posits a nature that is not a nature but a temple, a forest that is not a forest but an assembly of symbols. It is a mode of speech which corresponds to the possibility that Blanchot envisions as narration and writing: "Mais il se pourrait que raconter (écrire), ce soit attirer le langage dans une possibilité de dire qui dirait sans dire l'être et sans non plus le dénier" [But it might be possible that narrating (writing) could mean to draw language into a possibility of saying that would say being without saying it and yet not denying it].[35]

Baudelaire's forest of symbols, this forest full of echoes, posited as forest and yet other-than-forest (perhaps more forest than the forest), appears in Walter Benjamin's writing as symbol and innermost kernel of Language. The symbol "assumes meaning into its hidden and, if one may say so, forest-like interior."[36] If one may say so: the distant echo of Hölderlin's Rhein poem—"Denn weil/ Die Seligsten nichts fühlen von selbst,/Muß wohl, wenn solches zu sagen/Erlaubt ist, in der Götter Namen/Teilnehmend fühlen ein Andrer" [For because the most blissful ones feel nothing by themselves, it is necessary, if to say so is permitted, that another one must feel sympathetically in the name of the gods] (vv. 109–13)—indicates how precarious any saying is that wants to speak in the name of Language or in the name of the gods. Apparently such saying is possible only with a categorical reservation: if one may say so, if to say so is permitted. It can be said only by saying and not saying at the same time. It is unsaying, the furthest from soothsaying: *parole vide de paroles, écho toujours parlant au milieu du silence.*

The figure of language as forest and forest as language has the legitimation of a long tradition, reaching back to a time long before Baudelaire. It has been a topos of allegorical interpretation and its layers and levels of meaning at least since Gregory the Great, who figures explicitly the mountain forest as the topos of reading.[37] The so-called *silvae* (forests) were a special genre from the Renaissance to the baroque. Herder's *Kritische Wälder* still echoes the tradition in the second half of the eighteenth century. One of the most expansive and erudite works of this kind is the *Silva Allegoriarum Totius Sacrae Scripturae* of the Spaniard Hieronymus Lauretus (Jerónimo Lloret).[38] The two inclines of the allegorical mountain forest of language are clearly delineated here: on the one hand the *silva* indicates the unsystematic character of a work, a collection of various items (in this case an alphabetical order instead of a systematic order of things), emphasizing the allegorical power of dismembering and tearing apart the 'natural' world; on the other hand there is the claim for totality as a forest of the whole scripture (*Totius Sacrae Scripturae*). The latter claim is accompanied by another qualitative claim: to understand allegory in its highest— that is, spiritual-mystical—sense as a revelation beyond the rhetorical metaphor: "Sensus vero mysticus seu spiritualis est, quem Spiritus sanctus in rebus corporaliter aut gestis aut gerendis voluit significare" [The truly mystical or spiritual sense is that which the Holy Spirit wanted to signify bodily in things that happened or are about to happen].[39]

With this spiritual-mystical level of meaning, allegory turns into symbol in the sense in which Benjamin understood it in his early essays on language. It is a moment where the difference between metaphor and proper meaning is sublated in something different. The distance from 'metaphor' returns insistently in such moments: "The word 'language' is here not at all used in a metaphorical sense. For it is a fully substantial recognition that we cannot imagine anything that does not communicate its intelligible essence in expression,"[40] Benjamin writes in the essay "On Language in General and the Language of Man"; and in the essay on the task of the translator he wants to understand the thought of life and a continuation of the life of the work of art "in completely unmetaphorical objectivity [*Sachlichkeit*]."[41] *Sachlichkeit* is not the same as phenomenal reality; it is that which communicates itself as the intelligible being of the phenomena in language, just as, according to Lauretus, the Holy Spirit communicates itself in the *gestis*.

The Latin *gestus* reappears, semantically transformed, in the German *Gestus,* one of the key terms of Brecht's theater and the later Benjamin's concept of the symbol. Benjamin establishes the link between *Gestus* and symbol in contrast to parable and simile in his essay on Kafka: "Whereas the doctrinal content of Kafka's texts appears in the form of the parable, their symbolic content is enounced in the gesture [*Gestus*]. The actual antinomy of Kafka's work lies in the relation of simile and symbol."[42] The demonstrative theatricality and visibility of gesture stage the phenomenal world at the threshold of visibility: at the edges the visible world becomes blurred: "thus the most unforeseeable [*am unabsehbarsten*] thing for Kafka was certainly the gesture."[43] It is the demonstrative visibility of gesture that accounts for its "nebulous kernel" (*wolkiger Kern*). The word *unabsehbar* in German locates the limit of visibility not in the metaphysical difference of a visible surface and invisible ground but at the horizon of a visible surface, which is always visible in principle but at any given point limited by a horizon, where the phenomenal world vanishes: *à perte de vue,* as one says in French. The gesture as symbolic form transports the symbolic content from the invisibility of metaphysical depths into the expansive dissemination of a surface, limited only by a perspectival horizon. Thus the symbolic content is always visible in principle and always unattainable in principle like the legendary treasure at the end of the rainbow.

The individual gestures are joined together in the *Gestus* as an assembly of gestures. But just as the fragments of a vessel in Benjamin's simile remain the broken part of a vessel even when joined together, as Carol Jacobs rightly emphasized,[44] the *Gestus* remains a broken part. In the configurations of gestures the vertical lines of steps and arcades are flattened out again over the horizontal surface of contiguous parts and fragments. Their auditive version is the echo as refracted and fragmented voice, which might be re-assembled, as it is in some baroque echo plays, into a new frag-mentary sense.

The French translation of Benjamin's essay renders *Gefäß* (ves-sel) as *amphore,* which is perhaps an echo from the mouth of Beauty herself: "ta bouche une amphore" (Baudelaire, "Hymne à la beauté," v. 6). Derrida condenses the *amphore* with the meta-phor into an *ammétaphore*.[45] The neologism appropriately de-scribes the status of language in the echo space where everything is and is not, in the same way in which the hammering envisioned by Kafka is and is not: "to hammer together a table with the accu-racy and orderliness of an artisan and at the same time to do noth-ing, not in the sense that one could say 'hammering for him is noth-ing,' but rather 'hammering for him is a real hammering and at the same time also nothing,' in which case the hammering would have become even bolder, more decisive, more real, and, if you want, even crazier."[46]

In this throwing together of the amphora and the metaphor, the symbol—literally: that which is thrown together—is delineated as that which points at the relationship of all languages in pure Lan-guage and at the same time at the confusion of tongues in Babel:

> Comme de longs échos qui de loin se confondent
> Dans une ténébreuse et profonde unité
> Vaste comme la nuit et comme la clarté.

The unity of echoes in which the echoes melt together is the pure indifference of night and clarity, as it appears also in Baudelaire's dedication of the *Paradis artificiels* in the figure of the woman: "Toutefois il est évident que, comme le monde naturel pénètre dans le spirituel, lui sert de pâture, et concourt ainsi à opérer cet amalgame indéfinissable que nous nommons notre individualité, la femme est l'être qui projette la plus grande ombre ou la plus grande lumière dans nos rêves" [In any case it is evident that, just as the natural world penetrates into the spiritual world, serves as its pasture and thus brings about that undefinable concoction that we call our individuality, thus the woman is the being that projects the greatest shadow and the greatest light into our dreams].[47] The dark and profound unity of the languages in Language has its place in the name of Babel, which can be translated as "confusion." Thus it finds its echo in the *confuses paroles* of the "Correspondances"; and in the rhyme echo of *confondent* and *profonde* the profound unity resounds as the echo of Babel.[48]

It is at this point of indifference where "les transports de l'esprit et des sens" [the transports of the spirit and of the senses] take place. One might also locate here the transport from the metaphor to the *ammétaphore* in which the German ear can also hear the Platonic nurse, the *Amme* in Schleiermacher's translation of Plato's *Timaeus* (52d). This *Amme* is always already there "before": before the Law and before translation, shaking and shaken she hovers in space, in the Platonic *chôra;* thus she achieves the separation of the unseparated, the defining of the undefined.

The ammetaphor produces its effect of transports and definitions, the delineation of its figures, in space. This space is to be understood, according to the law of the ammetaphor, in unmetaphorical objectivity as a space of (re-)presentation, as graphematic space of writing, as a mountain forest of language, and as echo space of the ever newly refracted word. Benjamin's essay begins with an emphatic negation that is at the same time an emphatic positing of space: "Nirgends" [Nowhere]: nowhere, not never, spatially, not temporally, a line is delineated, a path against the path that leads astray ("vom Weg abführt" [4:9]).

To this *Nirgends*, the first negative determination of the essay, corresponds the echo of an empty "Dort" [There] in Benjamin's translation of Baudelaire's "Les aveugles": "Que cherchent-ils au Ciel, tous ces aveugles?" [What are they looking for in the Sky/Heaven, all these blind ones?].—"Was verrät sich Dort den Blinden?" [What betrays itself There to the blind ones?] (v. 14). The

French-capitalized "Ciel" becomes a capitalized "Dort" in the translation: a pure spatial direction. In Baudelaire's poetry "Ciel" is also the direction par excellence, although not without an ironic turn: "Vers le ciel quelquefois, comme l'homme d'Ovide, / Vers le ciel ironique et cruellement bleu" [Toward the sky sometimes, like the man of Ovid, toward the ironic and cruelly blue sky] ("Le cygne," vv. 25–26). The echo effect of the comparison *comme l'homme* resounds and vanishes in the emptiness which the name Ovid addresses: *O vide.*

Echolalia and the *écho toujours parlant au milieu du silence* begin to melt together in the direction and sense that Baudelaire's verses, his *vers,* indicate: a word that echoes through his poetry as verse, as worm, as direction and sense—the word that points at the emptiness of heaven and sky in the intention toward Language.

Benjamin insists on something that remains and lasts in all these versions and turns of direction and sense, precisely at the point where meaning becomes liquid: "Thus an ultimate, decisive element remains very close to and yet infinitely far away from [meaning], hidden underneath it, or more clearly refracted [*gebrochen*] through it, or more powerful beyond all communication. There remains in all language and in its formations outside of what is communicable something noncommunicable, something, depending on the context in which it is found, symbolizing or symbolized."[49] The work of separating, deciding, and defining, which is the work of the ammetaphor and the task of the translator, would thus arrive at an ultimate, decisive point that is neither sense nor nonsense. It stands in spatial, prepositional relations to sense and meaning: close to it, far from it, underneath it, through it, and beyond and over it. It seems most distant to it where conventional understanding most often looks for it: hidden underneath; more clearly—and thus closer to cognition—it appears where it is refracted, ruptured, in pieces (the multiply refracted echo of *Asia* in Hölderlin, the *confuses paroles* that look at man through the ammetaphoric forest and temple of the *correspondances*); its highest mode of presentation is presented as pure effect and power:

beyond all communication, Benjamin ascribes to it that powerful tangibility, which, according to Hölderlin, would be the condition that language can be anticipated and divined (*geahnt*). This is perhaps the decisive effect of all echoes, even in mere echolalia.

2. Recalling the Gods

Hölderlin
Baudelaire
Nietzsche

Dort bin ich, wo, wie Steine sagen Apollo gieng
In Königsgestalt.—Hölderlin

Hölderlin's texts resonate with the names and the naming of the ancient Greek gods, although it is above all the resonance of a profound absence. The naming of and the call to the absent produces a poetic and rhetorical force that can easily seduce readers and critics into a deceptive familiarity. One speaks of the gods as if one could speak of them and know of what one speaks.

Hölderlin's poetry puts this familiarity into question. An early poem chastises the "hypocritical poets" who speak of the gods and yet do "not believe in Helios, nor in the Thunderer and the Sea-god."[1] The poem addresses a situation in which the names of the Greek gods apparently have become mere rhetorical decoration. But what would it mean, as the poem suggests, to "believe" in Helios or, for that matter, in Dionysus and Apollo? The simple answer that it means to believe in their existence does not lead us very far. Even among believers the status of the object of faith extends over a wide range of conceptions.

Hölderlin's poem links the end of faith and the death of the earth to *Verstand* (analytic reason): "Ihr habt Verstand! ihr glaubt nicht." The poem points at a situation that Max Weber described later as the rationalization process of modernity that goes hand in hand with an irrevocable disenchantment and a demystification of the world. Hölderlin's invocation of the gods and, more than half a century later, Nietzsche's powerful invocation of Dionysus and Apollo as the figures of a rebirth of the gods in modernity might seem like a refusal of the irrevocability of the death of the gods that Baudelaire ridicules as a fake paganism of his time.

A closer reading of a few selected texts by Hölderlin, Baudelaire, and Nietzsche will unfold the difficulties and conditions of the reinvocation and significance of sacred names at the threshold of modernism when the significance of these names seems to have lost all legitimation and ground.

2

Commentators of Hölderlin sometimes try to differentiate his relationship to the names of the gods as something founded in "true experience" from a "mere allegorical" use of these names.[2] This distinction would presume to know both the nature of a "true experience" and the nature of "allegory." Neither can be taken for granted. If the names of the Greek gods, in particular Dionysus and Apollo, reemerged in the nineteenth century, stamping with a lasting effect the figures of modernity, the power of this effect is rooted less in the fullness of "true experience," as opposed to the merely allegorical, than in an allegorical staging of a loss of experience.

Indeed, it is not at all clear that Hölderlin's poem addressed to the "hypocritical poets" supports an opposition between believing in the names of the gods and their "mere allegorical" use. Although the poem does not go as far as acknowledging an explicit complicity with the hypocritical poets (as does Baudelaire's address to the hypocritical reader), its internal logic cannot detach itself from the emptiness that has marked the names of the gods.

The poetic voice that sets itself off so harshly in the first stanza through the interdictive imperative against the hypocritical poets ("You cold hypocrites, don't speak of the gods") cannot escape the problem of names that already are caught in the problem of *representing* something so fugitive that it might as well be nothing. The examples of the divine names given by the poem are symptomatic. The only Greek name in this poem is Helios. It is already on the threshold between name and concept: the word for "sun" and the sun god. It is followed by two German names or words: "Donnerer und Meergott" [Thunderer and Sea God]. The selection points at a reading of the names of the gods as figures of agents and forces of nature which, by the end of the eighteenth century, would not have been an unusual reading.

But the problem only begins here. Are we dealing with allegorical personifications, or, as some commentators emphatically insist, does Hölderlin's text aim at and achieve a radically different mode of representation? There is nothing that prevents us from reading "Helios" and "Donnerer und Meergott" as allegorical personifications. But there is the linguistic difference between the Greek name and the German words indicating a moment of transition and translation that is underlined by the grammatical shift from "Noch" [nor] to "und," separating Helios from the German couple "Donnerer und Meergott": "ihr glaubt nicht an Helios,/ Noch an den Donnerer und Meergott" [you do not believe in Helios,/Nor in the Thunderer and Sea God]. There is a rupture in the sequence of the three names. "You do not believe in Helios nor in the Thunderer and Sea God" can be read not only as a denial of faith in all of these gods but also as a denial of two different kinds of faith: belief in a Greek god as a mythical entity named Helios, and belief in a modern version of natural forces that might be representable in allegorical personifications like "Donnerer und Meergott." The denial of the latter possibility would be the more serious one, since it would remove the basis for translating the Greek names of the gods into a modern linguistic mode.

But there is still this Greek name: Helios denied by and forbidden to the hypocritical poets (*scheinheiligen Dichter*); yet he enters into a subversive relation with them, for not only is Helios the sun god who shines, the god of shining and appearance (and therefore already identified in ancient times with Apollo), but his Greek name also echoes the German word *heilig* ("holy").[3] He is thus indeed the god of the **schein-heiligen** *Dichter* and certainly the god of poets like Hölderlin, for whom the question of representation has become a problem.

The apparent neat division between the poetic voice and the hypocritical poets, between the implicit "I" or "we" of the poem and the emphatic plural "you" (*Ihr*), does not solve the problem of who could speak of the gods and in what manner. It is again the name Helios that points not so much at a solution but at the problem. The name of Helios is not only linguistically different from the German names "Donnerer und Meergott" (with which, on the other hand, it shares a certain affinity with a manifest allegorical personification), but it is also a name with a special distinction within the Greek pantheon. As the name of a visible natural phenomenon, the sun, Helios is different from names like Dionysus and Apollo, which have no direct connection to natural phenomena. Although there are other names and words in Greek mythology that share this double status of name and concept, Helios is distinguished with particular emphasis in the Sophoclean *Oedipus* when the chorus swears by him as "ton pantôn theon promon halion" (v. 660), which appears in Hölderlin's late translation of the plays as: "bei aller Götter/Vorläufer Helios" [by the predecessor of all gods, Helios] (FA 16:151). By translating *promos* as "predecessor," Hölderlin posits Helios not only in status but also temporally as the first of the gods.[4] As the god who precedes all other gods, he is outside the Olympian pantheon and yet in a determinate relation to it. But the determination is ambivalent: in the mythological tradition, Helios sometimes figures among the Titans who were replaced and literally covered up by the Olympian gods; but Helios is also the name of the most powerful natural phenomenon that shapes life on earth. In this sense, it is the name of a ground from which the names of the gods receive their living significance, the legitimating name of names. The two sides perhaps are not incompatible: the ground and its repression, the signifying force that emerges from the interdiction.

Hölderlin's late translation of Helios as predecessor of the gods is foreshadowed in the appearance of Helios in the earlier poem. The first stanza of the poem ends abruptly: "Todt ist die Erde, wer mag ihr danken?—" [Dead is the Earth, who can thank her?—]. Life and death of the earth are linked to the linguistic act of *danken* (to thank); for Hölderlin, this word is etymologically related to *denken* (to think) and epistemologically to *vorstellen* (to represent).[5] The ground of poetry is put into question, if not erased, by the dash that follows the question mark.

But out of this erasure emerges something like a consolation: "Getrost, ihr Götter! zieret ihr doch das Lied,/Wenn schon aus euren Nahmen die Seele schwand" [Be consoled, o you gods, you still adorn the song, although the soul has vanished from your names]. The "ihr" that referred to the hypocritical poets in the first stanza has become the "ihr" of the gods themselves. But the gods "themselves" are mere adornments, rhetorical flowers, names without a soul. The "ihr" of the personalizing address is the echo of adornment: ihr . . . *zieret ihr.* The consolation offered to the gods is addressed to the void itself that calls for the consolation. The poem acknowledges the void of the names from which the soul has vanished. And yet poetry needs not just words but a "great word": "Und ist ein großes Wort vonnöthen, / Mutter Natur! so gedenkt man deiner" [And if a great word is needed, Mother Nature! one remembers you]. Instead of empty names, the necessity of a "big" or "great word" arises. Rhetoric is often made of big words. But whether a *großes Wort* is merely a "big word" or a "great word," testifying to another significance, or perhaps belonging to the category referred to in French as *les gros mots,* remains an open question. The cathartic or aggressive violence of swear words and four-letter words might have more relevance for Hölderlin's *großes Wort* than pious invocations of "true experience." To the degree that their violence still functions in everyday speech acts, they testify to the power of taboos beyond any explicit individual act of faith and belief.

The poem appeals to a need or necessity. According to Hölderlin's "Fragment of a Philosophical Letter," it is precisely the moment when the speaking being rises above need and necessity that "thankfulness" and *Vorstellung* (representation) take place: "daß der Mensch auch in so fern sich über die Noth erhebt, als er sich seines Geschiks *erinnern,* als er für sein Leben *dankbar* seyn kann" [that man rises above necessity insofar as he can remember his fate, as he can be thankful for his life] (see note 5). In the poem, the need activates an act of remembrance: *danken* has been transformed into *gedenken* (remembering) as the condition of the "great" word.

"Mother Nature" irrupts into the series of addresses to the hypocritical poets and to the gods as an apostrophe, which is literally a turning away by turning to something else. From the empty names of the gods memory turns to and addresses "Mother Nature." Nature seems to provide the ultimate ground from which the names and the words regain significance, making possible the "great word." This reading would be supported by many of Hölderlin's texts in which the term "Nature" is given a privileged position. In the Pindaric ode "Wie wenn am Feiertage . . . ," Nature is posited explicitly above and before the gods:

Denn sie, sie selbst, die älter denn die Zeiten
Und über die Götter des Abends and Orients ist,
Die Natur ist jezt mit Waffenklang erwacht

[For she, she herself who is older than time and above the gods of the occident and orient, Nature is awakened with the sound of arms]. (vv. 21–23)

The position of Nature here is similar to that of Helios, whose name now appears as a synecdoche of the "great word," "Nature."

But who still believes in Helios? In another synecdoche of Nature, the Earth is declared dead, and it is her death that suspends the possibility of thankfulness and thinking, of memory and representation.

The apostrophe to "Mother Nature" neither guarantees a new faith in Helios nor revives the Earth. But the "great word" seems to depend on this apostrophe and its *gedenken*. It must then be something of a different order than the sum total of natural elements; it must be of a different order than Helios and the Earth, who no longer can inspire word or name.

In its search for a predecessor of the gods and an ultimate guarantor for the significance of their now soulless names, the poem arrives at a curiously bland, almost banal figure: Mother Nature. In the second half of the eighteenth century, "Nature" had become a privileged term of German poetry and poetics. German poets and critics had invoked "Nature" as a cosmic power, as a generative force, and as the very substance of genius and *Genie*. But it is precisely the fact that Hölderlin does not invoke "Nature" but "Mother Nature" that seems rather bland in comparison to the usual rhetorical flourishes of pantheistic cosmic invocations. The all-too-familiar family figure of the mother curiously detracts from the cosmic and omnipotent genius fantasies and introduces something more troubling.

Hölderlin's poem appeals less to the presence of a living nature (the Earth, after all, is dead) than to the memory (*gedenken*) of a topos presented in an allegorical figure. This figure, "the age-old Mother of All," once might have been, as Ernst Robert Curtius claims, "one of the last religious experiences of the late-pagan world";[6] but even if that was the case, it cannot be recaptured in the commonplace or topos that "Mother Nature" has become.

Commonplaces are not inherently without power; on the contrary, any skillful politician or advertising artist recognizes them as very powerful devices. The most worn-out coin will pay as well as the shining newly coined one, as long as it is kept in circulation by the order that stamped it. By the end of the eighteenth century (Hölderlin's poem was published in 1798), the rhetorical and poetological valorizations would support the pathos of an invocation to "Nature" ("Natur! Natur!" was the poetic battle cry of Goethe and others), but a figure like "Mother Nature" in its undisguised allegorical appearance was a challenge to the core of an aesthetic credo that opposed the genuine poetic symbol to the "merely allegorical."[7]

The familiarity of the word *mother* that imposes an allegorical stamp on the figure of nature also has its strange side. Goethe staged its plural in the second part of *Faust* as the strangest of all words situated in a place—or rather a nonplace—before all words and figures, a word with the uncanny effect of shudder: *Mütter* (mothers). Faust is struck by the word, and, most strangely, Mephisto calls it a "new word" (*neues Wort*), as if it had never been pronounced before. This staging of a most familiar word as strange and unknown performs a linguistic effect that Karl Kraus once described in the following formula: the closer one looks at a word, the more distantly it looks back. Children know the effect when they repeat a word over and over again until it has receded into the unreachable distance of a pure and strange sound vibrating with potential menacing and promising meanings. "The word grins," as Benjamin writes, when we look at it, as a pure word, as a skeleton, as a signifier, separated from the signified.[8]

Yet it remains this specific word, *Mutter,* with its plural *Mütter.* Faust gains access to it with an unmistakably obscene key, a "little thing" that quickly grows as Faust grasps it with his hand. At the threshold of desemantization, where the stability and petrification of meaning are shattered by the shudder of the uncanny (*Mütter* echoes with *erschüttern*), semantic ghosts hover. The word *Mutter/Mütter* continues to produce the phantoms of its semantics: the shudders of the sexual taboos, the interdictions and the phantasies of omnipotence.

Hölderlin's *Mutter Natur* rises as a ghost from the dead earth and as an allegorical specter from a poetics that had been declared dead by the new aesthetics. The earth is often named as "mother" in Hölderlin's poetry, and the word *Mutter* is heavily invested with connotations of silence (*verschwiegen*), somberness, melancholy, and death, a series which, coincidentally, also describes allegory in the rhetoric of the time.[9]

According to Walter Benjamin, the origin of European allegory is decisively linked with the dissolution of the pantheon of the ancient gods.[10] The Greek pantheon did not simply enter into a peaceful allegorization, where the names of the gods could be translated into representations and figurations of concepts. They entered the Christian hell, from where they kept returning as haunting ghosts, menacing demons, and sad figures of a lost serenity. Far from being 'cold' conceptual equations and pure products of analytical reason, the allegories that arise from the dissolved pantheon haunt Western rhetoric and poetics and are riddled with anxieties.

To name the gods is to name something forbidden, lost, and irretrievable, something that issues threats and promises at the same time. Instead of symbolic presence, it is allegorical anxiety that invests Hölderlin's poetry with a unique rhetorical and poetic intensity. Allegorical anxiety shapes the figures of his gods, interlaced with the familiar family figures that appear in the somberly connotated word *mother* and the serenely phantasized *father*.

3

An interdiction was directed at the hypocritical poets: "Don't speak of the gods." Several years later, in the poem "Germanien," it seems to return, addressed to the poet himself:

Nicht sie, die Seeligen, die erschienen sind,
Die Götterbilder in dem alten Lande,
Sie darf ich ja nicht rufen mehr

[Not them, the blissful ones, who once appeared, the divine images in the old land, I may no longer call them]. (vv. 1–3)

The force of the interdiction seems stronger than ever. The poetic subject itself stands under the force of an anonymous interdiction: "darf ich ja nicht" [I may not, I am not permitted to call them].

The interdiction is linked to a specific condition: they "who once have appeared, the divine images," may no longer be called. It is a double condition of an ontological status (the gods have *appeared*) and of a temporal one (they *have* appeared and are no longer apparent). The end of the first stanza underlines this pastness and the death of the gods. Whereas the beginning of the stanza does not address directly the gods who have appeared, but speaks of them in the third person, the end of the stanza turns to them directly in an apostrophe. But these gods are past and dead ones:

Und rükwärts soll die Seele mir nicht fliehn
Zu euch, Vergangene! die zu lieb mir sind.
Denn euer schönes Angesicht zu sehn,
Als wärs, wie sonst, ich fürcht' es, tödtlich ists,
Und kaum erlaubt, Gestorbene zu weken

[And my soul must not flee backwards, to you, past ones! who are too dear to me. For to see your beautiful face, as if it were as before, I am afraid, it is deadly, and hardly permitted to awaken the dead]. (vv. 12–16)

Trying to see what once entered into appearance is trying to see the face of the dead, conjuring deadly phantoms.

The old land as the place of appearance has disappeared, and the present land, the homeland of the poetic voice, is first addressed as water rather than land in the apostrophe "Ihr heimatlichen Wasser [You waters of the homeland]. Liquidity contrasts with the firmness of the old shaped land of appearances. The present land is the land of waters longing for something else, a no place, looking for a place; it is empty and full of expectations (*voll Erwartung*). It is ominously overshadowed:

> als in heißen Tagen
> Herabgesenkt, umschattet heut
> Ihr Sehnenden! uns ahnungsvoll ein Himmel.
> Voll ist er von Verheißungen und scheint
> mir drohend auch

[as in hot days, lowered down, full of forebodings a sky overshadows us. Full is it of promises and appears yet also menacing to me]. (vv. 7–11)

In the simulation of the "als in heißen Tagen," promises (*Verheißungen*) are formed. They also suggest promises of naming (*heißen* = to name, to be named, to have a name) in the form of shades that cover the light and diminish the heat. The truth effect of the German prefix *ver-*, in its capacity to displace the verbal activities on which it infringes, causing them to slip into another *veritas,* turns the simulated hotness (*heißen*) into a delayed promise (*Verheißungen*), the naming into a shading, and the shining appearance into the appearance of a menace.

It is as if phenomenality and seeing were irrevocably linked to the phenomenality of the Greek gods and among them to the shining god par excellence, Phoibos Apollo. Seeing becomes threatening. In his letter to Böhlendorff dated December 1801, Hölderlin writes: "O friend! the world lies brighter before me than before. . . . In earlier times I could jubilate about a new truth, about a better view of that which is above us and around us, now I am afraid it might happen to me what happened to old Tantalus who received a bigger share of the gods than he could digest" (StA 6:427). Several months later, after a brief stay in Bordeaux, Hölderlin seems to have seen too much. He writes to Böhlendorff again, after his return, that he has "seen the sad lonely earth; the shepherds of southern France and individual beauties, men and women, grown

up in the anxiety of patriotic doubt and hunger." But all this seeing stands under the verdict: "I may well say, as it has been said of
heroes, that I have been struck by Apollo" (StA 6:432).

The poem "Germanien" begins with the acknowledgment of
the irrevocable disappearance of appearance and ends with a command to name:

> Und nenne, was vor Augen dir ist,
> Nicht länger darf Geheimniß mehr
> Das Ungesprochene bleiben,
> Nachdem es lange verhüllt ist

[And name what is before your eyes, the unspoken must no longer
remain secret after having been veiled for a long time]. (vv. 83–86)

> Muß zwischen Tag und Nacht
> Einsmals ein Wahres erscheinen.
> Dreifach umschreibe du es,
> Doch ungesprochen auch, wie es da ist,
> Unschuldige, muß es bleiben

[Once, with one mark, something true must appear between day
and night. Threefold you must circumscribe it, but unspoken also,
as it is there, o innocent one, it must remain]. (vv. 92–96)

> O nenne Tochter du der heiligen Erd'
> Einmal die Mutter

[O name, you daughter of the holy earth, once your mother]. (vv.
96–97)

The command to circumscribe the unspoken threefold is performed in the threefold repetition and variation of the command,
indicating the complexity of naming. The first command aims at a
straightforward naming and unveiling of the unspoken. The second command seems to take this back: the unspoken must at the
same time remain unspoken "as it is there"; and while it must appear, its phenomenality is at the same time relegated into a twilight

zone "between day and night." In the third command, the naming not only seems to be reasserted again but also performed in the name of the earth and mother. But, coming after the second command, the status of this name is suspended in the twilight of the spoken and unspoken, of an appearance that is 'it' and not 'it': allegory in the most literal sense, saying 'it' by saying something else.

The name to be named, if it is a name at all, the name of the 'mother', the name of the 'earth' is, like the name of the one to whom the command is addressed, the daughter, named in the title as "Germanien," the most precarious, unstable, dated element of the poem. Far from rooting the text in a stable significance, these names and all-too-familiar family relations, and the acts committed in the name of Germanien, threaten the very survival of the text.[11] The poem is at the furthest distance from its center at the moment when it seems on the verge to name the unspoken.

If the text survives, precarious and vulnerable, it is to the degree that the poem unfolds the movement from the realization of the vanished phenomenality to the urgency of a naming that it can yet not achieve. The poem is this movement and has its place as the appearance of something true "between day and night," between the light of Helios, the vanished shining light of Phoibos Apollo, and something else, some other coming god. In order for something true to come again into appearance *Einsmals* ("at one time in the future," but also "with one mark"), the phenomenality of *damals* (at that time in the past), of that particular mark of the past, has to disappear.[12] The urgency of naming is intimately linked to the vanishing of the phenomenal presence in the "old land." Its "temple and image and also its customs" have gone from the "old land" to the "dark land" (vv. 22 ff.). Only a "golden smoke" remains of the luminosity of the former appearances, but this smoke is also already *die Sage,* "the legend" and, more literally, "the saying."

At this moment, another transition takes place. The personal voice of the mourning *ich,* the privileged locus of lyrical sentiment in Hölderlin's time, is erased. The golden smoke of the *Sage* from the tomb of the past produces a twilight around "us" ("und dämmert jezt uns Zweifelnden ums Haupt"). The multiplication of the first person singular into the plural is at the same time its erasure: "Und keiner weiß" [and no one knows]. But precisely in this erasure of the personal voice, the past becomes, in Hölderlin's poetological term, *fühlbar*. It can be felt: "Er fühlt/Die Schatten derer, so gewesen sind" [He feels the shadows of those who have been]. The new pronoun "He" refers to "keiner": through this placeholder of no one something like an experience takes place. It is here where the pastness of the past is transformed into the urgency of something to come: "Denn die da kommen sollen, drängen uns" [For they who are supposed to come urge us] (v. 30).

They who are supposed to come are the ancients and yet not the same as the ancients: in coming, they point back to an appearance that has been and is now irrevocably lost. While the figure of the phenomenality of the gods coalesces in the figure of Helios/Phoibos/Apollo, the figure of the coming one who points back is Dionysus: "Dorther kommt und zurük deutet der kommende Gott" [From there he comes and backward points the coming god] ("Brod und Wein," v. 54). Hölderlin takes Dionysus at his word; the first word that he pronounces in the *Bacchae* of Euripides is *hêkô*: "I come." What is now coming in the words of the poem is indeed marked by the signs of Dionysus, beginning with the "waters of the homeland," for water, not only wine, signals the dissolving, liquidating power of Dionysus. In his self-presentation in the *Bacchae*, which Hölderlin partly translated, he points back at his fiery origin in the lightning bolt that blasted Semele (*lochtheis' astrapêphorô pyri*, v. 3). He differentiates that origin from his present *parousia* at the waters of Dirke and Ismenos: *pareimi Dirkês namat' Ismênou th'hydôr* (v. 5).[13] For Hölderlin, the association with water is a crucial element for the Dionysian polysemic dissemination in the production of name and language.[14] In Hölderlin's *Antigone* translation, Dionysus with the many names (*polyônyme*) becomes the one who gives and creates the names: *Nahmenschöpfer*. The waters of the homeland that mark absence and longing at the beginning of the poem later merge together with the fullness of the "golden word" ("Doch Fülle der goldenen Worte sandtest du auch/Glükseelige! mit den Strömen und sie quillen unerschöpflich" [vv. 73–74]). This golden word in turn emerges from the "golden smoke" (v. 25) as the *Sage* of the disappeared appearances.

The smoke from the ashes of the divine images is both saying (*Sage*) and legend ("to be read"). Emerging from the ashes of Semele, Dionysus comes into his present appearance (*pareimi*) at the waters of Ismenos and mingles there, through another text, which Hölderlin translated, with the prophesying ashes of Apollo Ismenos in the Sophoclean Oedipus: *ep' Ismênou te manteia spodô* (v. 21).

The command "to name what is before your eyes" is preceded by the command "to drink"—"O trinke Morgenlüfte" (v. 81)— and followed by a tempestuous liquification:

Es rauschen die Wasser am Fels
Und Wetter im Wald und bei dem Nahmen derselben
Tönt auf aus alter Zeit Vergangengöttliches wieder

[The waters rush on the rocks and the weathers in the woods, and, at the name of her, past divineness resounds again up from ancient times]. (vv. 98–100)

The *rauschen* of the water not only evokes the disarticulation of distinct tones into the blurred noises of rushing and roaring but also the word *Rausch:* intoxication. Tones reemerge from the disarticulation and intoxication to remind us that Hölderlin's poetics is founded on a theory of systematically alternating "tones": "Tönt Vergangengöttliches wieder." The Apollonian images that have disappeared return transformed into another medium as the tones that are associated through the *rauschen* with the figure of Dionysus.

But what is this name, "bei dem Nahmen derselben": the name of her, herself, the same one? There is some grammatical ambivalence here, for technically *derselben* could also be a plural and refer to the names of the waters rushing on the rock. But the context strongly suggests another reading. The name to be named is the name of the mother: "O nenne Tochter der heiligen Erd'/Ein-

mal die Mutter" [O name, daughter of the holy earth, once your
mother] (vv. 97–98).

As in the earlier poem, it is again the name of the mother which
is supposed to guarantee the possibility of a naming or renaming
of the gods; it allows the divineness of the name to resound. The
word "mother" is introduced with great rhetorical emphasis:

> Denn fast wie der heiligen,
> Die Mutter ist von allem, und den Abgrund trägt
> Die Verborgene sonst genannt von Menschen

[For almost like of the holy one, who is the mother of all and bears
the abyss, formerly named the hidden one by men]. (vv. 75–77)

This mother of all remains curiously elusive. The verses are addressed to the daughter, Germania, an allegorical persona who is
said to be "almost" as full of love, suffering, and divination as the
mother. When the daughter of the earth, Germania, is asked to
name the mother once, can it be said that the poem names the
name of the mother by addressing the "daughter of the holy
earth"? Is the name of the mother *Erd'* (earth)? According to the
earlier poem to the hypocritical poets, the earth is dead, and
Mother Nature must be invoked for the great word to be possible.
If her name were "earth," why should she have been called "the
hidden one"? Rather than being the name of the mother, earth is
perhaps simply earth to cover up something, another screen word
for the name that is not named but only promised. Earth, then, is
as much an allegory as "Germania."

But like the word *mother*, the word *Erde* is a specific word that
seems to elicit shudders even (or perhaps particularly) in philological souls. The long entry on *Erde* in Grimm's *Deutsches Wörterbuch* begins with a gesture of awe and mystery: "eines so durch-
greifenden, altverjährten wortes ursprung verliert sich im dunkel"
[the origin of such a far-reaching, age-old word fades into dark-
ness]. The Germanic variants of *ërda* are presented as an inversion
and displacement of the Latin *terra*.[15] The word seems to emerge
through a movement of inversion from the darkness of an abyss.

Aside from Hölderlin's singular and private investments in the words *Erde* and *Mutter,* they resonate in his poetry with a linguistic history and dimension that point beyond the horizon of the individual.

The invocation of a hidden and perhaps dead mother as the precondition for the recalling of the newly coming gods under the signs of Dionysus also has a basis in the *Bacchae* of Euripides. When Dionysus comes to Thebes, he emphasizes this coming as a return to the memorial place of his mother (*mêtros mnêma,* v. 6). It has been made into a sacred, untouchable, and inaccessible ground (*abaton . . . pedon,* v. 10) by Cadmus, to the great satisfaction of Dionysus, who himself covered and hid it (*ekalupsa*) with vines.

Hölderlin, who later renamed Dionysus as the "creator of names," rewrites the problem of naming under the signs of Dionysus. The name of the mother is the name of a taboo: its simultaneous naming and not naming is the precondition of any naming. It points at a *Grund* (ground) before the *Abgrund* and deeper than the *Abgrund.* It bears the abyss: "Die Mutter ist von allem, und den Abgrund trägt."[16]

The appearance of the signs of Dionysus at the crucial moment of the naming of the "unspoken" through the mystery of the name of the mother and the earth points toward Dionysus as the privileged figure of naming. He is the key figure of the poem "Bread and Wine" (originally entitled "Der Weingott" [God of Wine]); the poem unfolds the scenario of the foundation of the sign from the Eleusinian mysteries to the Last Supper. Yet he is not named but only signaled and circumscribed in his epithets and emblems (God of Wine, pine tree, ivy): he is the hidden figure of figures. In addition, the change of the title from "God of Wine" to "Bread and Wine" alludes to the symbolic reorganization that took place through Christianity; it displaced the Olympian gods as they displaced the Titans. At the end of the poem the signs of Dionysus merge with the figure of Christ, who appears as "Fakelschwinger des Höchsten/Sohn, der Syrier" [the torchbearer, son of the Highest, the Syrian] (vv. 155 f.).

The merging of Dionysus and Christ is not without a foundation in the text of Euripides *après coup*. Dionysus presents himself
emphatically as the god who has taken human shape: *morphên
d'ameipsas ek theou brotêsian* (v. 4), a formulation that must have
resonated strongly for Hölderlin, a former student of theology.
Even more striking is Tiresias's description of the new god Dionysus as the one who "is poured out as a libation to the gods being
a god himself" (*houtos theoisi spendetai theos gegôs*, v. 284). The
effect of the *après coup*, where elements of a former symbolic organization are rearranged and given other meaning in a new organization of the symbolic material, is here overdetermined by the
fact that the Paulinian letters seem to echo the Euripidean language, when Paul writes to Timothy, "Egô gar êdê spendomai" [I
namely will soon be poured as a libation] (2 Tim. 4:6), a formulation that is further echoed in Phil. 2:17.[17]

In contrast to some commentators, Hölderlin does not simply
translate Dionysus into Christian and eucharistic terms. He stages
instead the conflictual interplay between the symbolic orders as the
actual subject of the elegiac poetic process. A common German epi-
thet for Christ is *Gottmensch*, a direct translation of the church
fathers' *theantrôpos* or *theandros;* it appears as early as medieval
German, and it became common usage in the mid-eighteenth century.[18] Hölderlin provocatively transforms the word into the plural
Göttermenschen in the poem "Germanien": "Und länger säumt
von Göttermenschen / Die heilige Schaar nicht mehr im blauen
Himmel" [And no longer lingers the holy swarm of godmen in the
blue sky] (vv. 30 ff.). Although the Greek gods as they appeared—
as *Götterbilder* (god images)—can no longer be called, they will
return as *Göttermenschen*.

This shift from the ancient Apollonian phenomenality of the
gods as *Götterbilder* to the possibility of a modern reappearance
in the Dionysian/Christian phenomenality of *Göttermenschen* sets
up the scenario for the translations of modernity by Baudelaire and
Nietzsche. Hölderlin's *Göttermenschen* performs a double translation: he translates the *Götterbilder* that have disappeared into
the symbolic order of the Christian *Gottmensch*, and he retrans-

lates this monotheistic figure into the polytheistic figure of *Göttermenschen*. The translation emphasizes two points: the impossibility of ever returning to a symbolic structure that has undergone a radical transcription and reorganization, and at the same time the haunting reappearance of the former symbolic elements.

What does Hölderlin read in the Euripidean Dionysus and his incarnation in the *morphên . . . brotêsian*? It is a commonplace of cultural histories that the achievement of the Greeks consisted in a unique humanization of the gods and that in their art the interpenetration of the human and the divine formed the foundation of true humanism. The Greek gods are indeed human, all too human in every respect, except one: they are immortal. Although they may share every human frailty, desire, and lust, an abyss separates them as immortals from the mortals. Hölderlin translates the *morphên . . . brotêsian* as "sterbliche Gestalt an Gottes statt annehmend" [assuming mortal shape instead of god's] (FA 17:628–29).

Prefigured not only in the Euripidean *morphên . . . brotêsian* but also in the Orphic Dionysus Zagreus and in Heraclitus's identification of Dionysus and Hades,[19] this entry into mortality now emerges as the figure of the possibility of a coming god, one who will come again: a revenant. The Gestalt of this god is the modern body, marked by a new organization of the symbolic and imaginary structures that determine the relation to death and sexuality.

Already Hölderlin figures the radical difference between antiquity and modernity in the relation to death, more specifically to the dead body, to the corpse. In his letter to Böhlendorff in December 1801 he describes the modern tragic form in terms of modern burial customs. In contrast to the Greeks, whose bodies were consumed by the flames that they could not contain, we "go away from the realm of the living very quietly packed up in some container" (StA 6:426). Following Hegel and Nietzsche, Benjamin marks the turning point in the death of Socrates. In Socrates the relationship of mortality and immortality enters into a new structure: "Socrates looks death in the eyes like a mortal—like the best, the most virtuous of the mortals—but he recognizes in death something foreign beyond which, in immortality, he expects to find himself again."[20] Death is exterritorialized into the alien territory of an estranged body.

Struck by Apollo, as he writes to Böhlendorff after his return from Bordeaux, Hölderlin sees the athletic bodies of southern France. But the gaze of the seer first encounters the primal vision of 'mother' earth: "I have seen the sad lonely earth," the letter begins. This vision of the sad mother who bears the melancholic abyss of the seer is as much the condition for his being struck by Apollo as Apollo's striking is the condition for a new vision. Like Dionysus, Apollo reemerges in the modern figuration of death and sexuality mediated through the figure of mother earth. The constellation is emblematically and enigmatically inscribed on a page in the Homburger folio (containing the major late poems and fragments of Hölderlin): "Zwei Bretter und zwei/Brettchen apoll envers terre."[21] In the minimalized coffin of two boards and two little boards,[22] the Apollonian phenomenality appears in the emphatic duality of two languages and two sexes: the "individual beauties" of "men and women."

The refiguration of Dionysus and Apollo as a refiguration of sexuality and death in the name of the mother is perhaps the most striking parallel symbolic event to the transition from Oedipus to Hamlet.[23] Freud describes the shift from Oedipus to Hamlet as a "secular progression in repression."[24] What appeared once in the light ("ans Licht gezogen") of Helios and Phoibos Apollo is now hidden in the "dark light" of the new Dionysian wine of remembrance.[25] It is this structure of *Verborgenheit*, of veiling and revelation and revelation in veiling, which produces the particular hide-and-seek of the gods, their *fort-da* play in Hölderlin's poetry.

At the pivot of this structure is the hidden mother, "Die Verborgene sonst genannt von Menschen," who commands the taboo and its revelation, what must not be called ("Sie darf ich ja nicht rufen mehr") and what must be called ("Nicht länger darf Geheimniß mehr/Das Ungesprochene bleiben"). The result is a rewriting through detours: circumscription ("Dreifach umschreibe du es") around the unspoken ("Doch ungesprochen auch, wie es da ist,/Unschuldige, muß es bleiben").

The rewriting affects the structure of (re-)presentation itself. Past divineness resounds again at the naming of her name; the divinity of Dionysus and Apollo enters the scene of modernity as a privileged power: they are the figures of representation in modernity wherever they reemerge in more than decorative form. While Nietzsche's recall staged their shaping force of modern *Darstellung* most visibly, a lesser-known text of Baudelaire articulates another side of the ongoing mourning process of the Greek gods.

4

In his *Ecole Païenne,* Baudelaire remarks with ironic astonishment that a young man offers a toast to the god Pan at a banquet celebrating the February Revolution.[26] Asked what Pan has to do with the revolution, the young man self-confidently announces that Pan is the revolution. He is not disturbed by the objection that Pan has long been dead, a pronouncement that according to Plutarch resonated throughout the Mediterranean region and which Baudelaire's text echoes in capital letters: "LE DIEU PAN EST MORT."

Baudelaire seems all the more disturbed about a curious lack of its acknowledgment among his contemporaries, who, despite their avowed paganism, seemed to be deaf to that resonating voice of the death of the god and the gods. The initial mocking and ironic tone of Baudelaire's text soon yields to a rather heavy pathos of what seems like moral outrage. But one should not too quickly label the source of this disturbance that permeates the text. The tone of moral outrage might be one of the textual waves created by a more profound disturbance whose source is yet to be located.

If the mocking tone is directed at a "folie, innocente en apparence," the more severe rhetoric aims at something more dangerous. Baudelaire's polemic inverts a poetic tradition which, since the late eighteenth century, invoked the Greek gods in the name of aesthetic sensuality and beauty against the somber repressions of Christianity. Schiller's poem "Die Götter Griechenlands" (1788–1800) set the tone not only in Germany but also in France, where Musset's elegiac question "Regrettez-vous le temps où le ciel sur la terre / Marchait et respirait dans un peuple de dieux" [Do you regret the time when heaven walked on earth and breathed in a people of gods] still found an echoing answer in Rimbaud's "Soleil et chair": "O Vénus, ô Déesse!/Je regrette les temps de l'antique jeunesse" [O Venus, o goddess! I regret the times of ancient youth].[27] The appeal to the Greek gods is made in the name of an aesthetics of sensual and spiritual harmony that claims to be the foundation of art and literature.

But no less is at stake in Baudelaire's violent inversion: "Congédier la passion et la raison, c'est tuer la littérature. Renier les efforts de la société précédente, chrétienne et philosophique, c'est se suicider, c'est refuser la force et les moyens de perfectionnement" [To dismiss passion and reason means to kill literature. To deny the efforts of the preceding Christian and philosophical society means to commit suicide] (p. 47). The rhetoric of killing and suicide is emphatically repeated as the threat of "une littérature homicide et suicide" in the last words of the essay. In contrast to a powerful aesthetic tradition Christianity does not threaten art, but its denial is posited as the deadly threat. While Marx declared religion (above all, Christianity) as the opium for the people, Baudelaire declares the new paganism as the opium for the writer: "cette déplorable manie, qui tend à faire de l'homme un être inerte et de l'écrivain un mangeur d'opium" [this deplorable mania that tends to turn man into an inert being and the writer into an opium consumer].

Baudelaire's gesture seems directed against more than just a fad: something at the core of art and literature, and certainly something different from faith in a positive religion, is at stake. Indeed, when *tuer* and *suicider* reappear at the end as the threat of *homicide et suicide*, Christianity has disappeared and the *société précédente, chrétienne et philosophique* has been replaced by a future one (*Le temps n'est pas loin*) in which literature must march between *la science et la philosophie* if it wants to survive.

The entrance of science at this point seems strange after Baudelaire's condemnation of a materialist reduction of beauty in the paganist rhetoric: "S'environner exclusivement des séductions de l'art physique, c'est créer de grandes chances de perdition. Pendant longtemps, bien longtemps, vous ne pourrez voir, aimer, sentir que le beau . . . dans un sens restreint. . . . . Le monde ne vous apparaîtra que sous sa forme matérielle" [To surround oneself exclusively with the seductions of sensual art means to create good chances for ruin. For a long time, for a very long time, you will be able to see, to love, to feel only the beautiful . . . in a very narrow sense. . . . The world will appear to you only in its material form]. But Baudelaire invokes another materiality against the pagan statues and images: "Toutes ces statues de marbre seront-elles des femmes dévouées au jour de l'agonie, au jour du remords, au jour de l'impuissance?" [All these marble statues, will they be devoted women on the day of agony, on the day of remorse, on the day of impotence?]. The pathos of the rhetorical question points at a body other than the one represented by classical sculpture, which, since Winckelmann and Hegel, had become the embodiment of classical beauty.

Baudelaire confronts the classical statues with a body marked by death and torn by antagonisms (*agonie*), by guilt (*remords*), and by a sexuality stamped with the negativity of impotence and castration (*impuissance*). Baudelaire's modern body is in this particular sense a Christian body; the word *passion* is heavily invested with the connotation of suffering, the passion as the path to Calvary. Passion and reason enter into a curious relationship as pillars of literature: *Congédier la passion et la raison, c'est tuer la littérature.* But this is not the harmonious balance of nature and spirit that was imagined in the classical statues but rather the pathetic and even pathological antagonism of a Christian spirituality in the suffering body. Its poetological counterpart can be found in the antagonistic couple of *spleen et idéal.* That the *passion* is indeed a *passion chrétienne* is underlined by the parallelism of *la passion et la raison* and *société . . . chrétienne et philosophique.*

It is evidently not a question of a sentimental return to Christianity but rather the acknowledgment of the indelible power that a preceding social organization (*la société précédente, chrétienne et philosophique*) has exerted on the symbolic order and the subject's position in it. Any attempt simply to return to another organization such as the imagined serene sensuality and beauty of a pre-Christian pagan world and its gods would fall under Baudelaire's verdict of *sentimentalisme matérialiste*.[28]

When Bacchus does appear in Baudelaire's poetry, it is in the somber world of the *Femmes damnées* who scream to him feverishly, "Ô Bacchus, endormeur des remords anciens!" [O Bacchus, who puts to sleep ancient remorse].[29] In a curiously medieval move, the ancient gods have entered a Christian hell of remorse and guilt which they try in vain to put to sleep. In the *Spleen de Paris,* the figures of Bacchus and Satan melt into each other: "Le visage du premier Satan était d'un sexe ambigu, et il y avait aussi, dans les lignes de son corps, la mollesse des anciens Bacchus" [The face of the first Satan was of an ambiguous sex, and he also had in the traits of his body the softness of ancient Bacchus figures].[30] Baudelaire seems to revoke the rebirth of the Olympian gods in the Renaissance. But as Warburg and Panofsky demonstrated in the arts and as Benjamin has shown in the baroque *Trauerspiel,* that rebirth was always precarious and ambivalent.[31] While the German baroque emphasized the radical ambivalence of the mortal body, Baudelaire accentuates the troubling ambivalence of the sexual body in the figure of Bacchus/Satan.[32]

Benjamin locates three major relations through which the baroque reaches over and across the Renaissance into medieval Christianity: "the battle against the pagan gods, the triumph of allegory, the martyrdom of corporeality."[33] The ideological battle against the pagan gods is the visible staging of a symbolic organization marked by modern allegory and a structure of the imaginary obsessed with the tortured, mutilated body. These structures cause a radical rupture. The humanist invocation of the ancient gods and their beauty is overshadowed by the crucified body of Christ and the exquisitely tortured bodies of martyrs and saints that fill our art museums, in the same way Winckelmann's Belvedere Apollo is overshadowed by the systematically tortured sexual bodies of the Marquis de Sade that still haunt the screen of Pasolini's cinematic imagination.

5

Baudelaire's essay performs a baroque gesture to set the scene for a modernity that is indelibly marked by his poetry. This gesture seems to represent the extreme countergesture to Nietzsche's proclamation, two decades later, of the birth (or rebirth) of tragedy in the names of Dionysus and Apollo, who had been destroyed by philosophy (through Socrates), Christianity, and science.[34]

Yet the two gestures emerge from the same experience of a void and irrevocable loss. The profound anxiety of getting lost without return in the mourning memory of the gods, which is expressed in Hölderlin's poetry, turns into a diagnostic rhetorical question in Baudelaire's essay: "Vous avez sans doute perdu votre âme quelque part, dans quelque mauvais endroit, pour que vous couriez ainsi à travers le passé comme des corps vides pour en ramasser une de rencontre dans les détritus anciens?" [You have doubtlessly lost your soul somewhere, in some bad environment, since you run thus across the past like empty bodies in order to pick one up from the ancient refuse?] (p. 47). The writer himself cannot escape the magnetism of this void: "Il me semble que je fais un mauvais rêve, que je roule à travers le vide et qu'une foule d'idoles de bois, de fer, d'or et d'argent, tombent avec moi, me poursuivent dans ma chute, me cognent et me brisent la tête et les reins" [It seems to me that I am having a bad dream, that I am rolling across the void, and that a swarm of wooden, iron, golden, and silver idols are tumbling with me, pursue me in my plunge, knock and smash my head and loins] (p. 46). Baudelaire implicates his own body in the post-Socratic destruction of the beautiful body, which, according to Nietzsche, had already begun before Socrates: "Das ihm [Sokrates] eigenthümliche Element der Dialektik hat sich bereits lange Zeit vor Sokrates in das Musikdrama eingeschlichen und verheerend in dem schönen Körper gewirkt" [This element of dialectic, characteristic of Socrates, had sneaked into the musical drama long before him with devastating effects for the beautiful body] (1:545).

Nietzsche's writing of *The Birth of Tragedy* is a writing after and through Socrates' dialectics. It presupposes the death of tragedy and the gods and the void produced by that death: "Mit dem Tod des griechischen Musikdramas dagegen entstand eine ungeheuere, überall tief empfundene Leere" [With the death of the Greek musical drama an immense void, felt deeply everywhere, came into existence] (1:533). Not even a suicidal descent into the underworld could reach them any longer: "man würde sich getödtet haben, um noch mehr von ihm [Sophokles] zu lernen, wenn man nicht gewusst hätte, dass die tragischen Dichter ebenso todt seien als die Tragödie" [One would have killed oneself in order to learn more from Sophocles if one had not known that the tragic poets were as dead as tragedy itself] (1:536).[35] Like Baudelaire, Nietzsche evokes the death scream of the Greek gods: "der grosse Pan ist tot" [the great Pan is dead]; and he doubles it with his own variation: "die Tragödie ist tot" [tragedy is dead] (1:75). The recurring anxious question in Hölderlin's poetry—Where are the temples of the ancients?—is echoed in Nietzsche's text in a declaration of an irrevocable death: "der herrlichste Tempel liegt in Trümmern; was nützt uns die Wehklage des Zerstörers?" [the most magnificent temple lies in ruins; of what use is the lamentation of the destroyer?] (1:83).

Alternating between Dionysus and *Der Gekreuzigte* ("The Crucified"), Nietzsche's late signatures are foreshadowed underneath the Wagnerian propaganda in the elaboration of *The Birth of Tragedy*. Dionysus enters as the god of "passion" with the same overdetermined resonance of the word which occurred in Baudelaire's essay. Greek tragedy now appears as *Leidensgeschichte des Dionysus* (1:527), the Aristotelian pity becomes a *Mitleiden*, a suffering along with the suffering of the god.

The first appearance of the names of Apollo and Dionysus in *The Birth of Tragedy* transforms the names into adjectival forms: "die Duplicität des Apollinischen und Dionysischen" [the duplicity of the Apollonian and the Dionysian] (1:25). This adjectival transformation of the names is connected with a specific history of aesthetics which is marked in the late eighteenth century by the transformation of names of genres as specific literary forms (e.g., tragedy or elegy) into adjectival categories (the tragic or the elegiac). Rather than describing specific forms and techniques of poetic productions, these adjectival nouns refer to fundamental modes of being and their presentation.[36]

The adjectivization emerges from a rethinking of the question of *Darstellung,* of presentation itself. The duplicity through which Nietzsche introduces the Dionysian and Apollonian is not accidental; the structure of *Darstellung* itself is marked by the duplicity of a hidden ground and manifest appearance. This duplicity already structured Hölderlin's poetics as the duplicity of a musical *Grundton* (ground tone) and a manifest Gestalt as *Kunstcharakter* (artistic character).

In Nietzsche, the Dionysian and Apollonian become the figures of *Darstellung* or, more precisely, the figures of a specific thinking of *Darstellung* as the duplicity of a lost unity for which Schiller's division between the "naive" of the ancients and the "sentimental" of the moderns had provided a powerfully effective model. Lukács's *Theory of the Novel* still opens with the same scenario.

Nietzsche projects the duplicity itself into antiquity. From the beginning, in the earliest drafts of *The Birth of Tragedy,* the Greek naming and (re-)presentation are characterized by the duplicity of hiding and manifestation. Nietzsche speaks of "Die Griechen, die die Geheimlehre ihrer Weltanschauung in ihren Göttern aussprechen und zugleich verschweigen" [the Greeks who enounce and at the same time conceal in their gods the secret teaching of their world view] (1:553). Both Hölderlin and Nietzsche see tragedy as the presentation of an original fissure. But whereas Hölderlin emphasizes the presentation of division and struggle in tragedy as a representation of an original unity, Nietzsche projects the division into the unity itself. The original Oneness (*das Ur-Eine*) is already the eternal suffering one in its primal contradictions. Oneness, it seems, is already duplicity and contradiction: "dass das Ur-Eine, als das Ewig-Leidende und Widerspruchsvolle, zugleich die entzückende Vision, den lustvollen Schein zu seiner Erlösung braucht" [that the original One, the eternally suffering One, and the One full of contradictions needs simultaneously the raptured vision, the pleasureful appearance for its redemption]. Raphael's *Transfiguration* represents for Nietzsche the "Widerspiegelung des ewigen Urschmerzes, des einzigen Grundes der Welt: der Schein ist hier Widerschein des ewigen Widerspruchs, des Vaters der Dinge" [mirroring of the eternal primal suffering, of the only ground of the world: appearance here is a reflection of the eternal contradiction, the father of things] (1:38–39).

The original duplicity of the One in Nietzsche is the basis of his theory of representation and appearance that is figured in the duplicity of the Apollonian and the Dionysian. This primacy of the duplicity in the One gives another turn to the adjectival forms. Their claim to point beyond the empirical forms of genre to a fundamental mode of being, represented in the genre, is inverted: they point toward the irreducible primacy of representation and *Darstellung*. While Nietzsche's narrative seems to privilege on one level the traditional hierarchy of a latent ground that is represented in a manifest appearance (art as the phenomenalization of life), Nietzsche reads his own text in his *Versuch einer Selbstkritik* against its narrative and yet true to its logic, claiming that "all life rests on appearance, art, deception, optics, necessity of perspectivism, and of error" (1:18).

More important, however, than the hierarchies and their inversions is the structure of inversion itself which characterizes the figures of *Darstellung:* whatever is (re-)presented, 'put forth', 'translated', and 'expressed' is the opposite, the inversion of what 'it' is supposed to 'be'. In this structure, Nietzsche's philosophy coincides with Hölderlin's poetics.

Nietzsche presents the duplicity of the Dionysian/Apollonian *Darstellung* in a sexual analogy: "the further development of art is tied to the duplicity of the Apollonian and Dionysian in a similar way as generation depends on the duality of the sexes" (1:25). The analogy points toward another generating ground and scenario: the Medusa is not far away. The Apollonian erection must offer its apotropaic charm against her. Seeing the ground, seeing the truth is petrifying: "Sie anzuschaun macht zu Stein" (1:562). Naming the gods becomes a "Spiegel gegen die Meduse zu schützen" [a mirror to protect against the Medusa] (1:560). Nietzsche tells us in the version of the satyr what that truth is: the best thing being never to be born, the second best to die as soon as possible. One might read this as a desire for straight annihilation, for pure nothingness; but Nietzsche's text suggests another possibility. Never to be born could also mean to have never been separated from the mother: a figure that permeates Nietzsche's text and is, as we have seen also in Hölderlin, intricately linked to the vicissitudes of *Darstellung*. Nietzsche's first major work is the story of a birth: *Die Geburt der Tragödie aus dem Geist der Musik*. What is claimed as ground, the Dionysian music, gives birth to the abyss of human existence (just as in Hölderlin's poem the mother "bears the abyss": "Die Mutter ist von allem, und den Abgrund trägt"). Melody gives birth to poetry ("die Melodie gebiert die Dichtung aus sich"); the chorus sections are a maternal womb giving birth to the dialogues ("Jene Chorpartien, mit denen die Tragödie durchflochten ist, sind also gewissermaassen der Mutterschooss des ganzen sogenannten Dialogs") (1:62). If tragedy is the presentation of a primal suffering and passion, Oedipus, "the murderer of his father, the husband of his mother, Oedipus the solver of the riddle of the sphinx," is the most paradigmatic figure of this suffering ("die leidvollste Gestalt"). Nietzsche reads in Oedipus the "Dionysian wisdom" as the revelation of a "monstrous unnaturalness" (*eine ungeheuere Naturwidrigkeit*). The Dionysian wisdom emerges from incest with the mother: "dass dort, wo durch weissagende und magische Kräfte der Bann von Gegenwart und Zukunft, das starre Gesetz der Individuation und überhaupt der eigentliche Zauber der Natur gebrochen ist, eine ungeheure Naturwidrigkeit—wie dort der Incest— als Ursache vorausgegangen sein muss" (1:65–67).

At the kernel of modernity, there is a particular and troubling phantasy of the mother that is at the core of *Hamlet*. The mother is not a figure but a name and a word that produces figures, gives birth to the phenomenal world and makes possible the recall of the ancient gods, just as the realm of the mothers in Goethe's *Faust* is the precondition for the phenomenalization and the recalling of Helena. Nietzsche explicitly links the Dionysian jubilation with Goethe's "mothers": "während unter dem mystischen Jubelruf des Dionysus der Bann der Individuation zersprengt wird und der Weg

zu den Müttern des Seins, zu dem innersten Kern der Dinge offen-
liegt" [while the spell of individuation bursts under the mystical
jubilation of Dionysus and the path to the mothers, to the innermost kernel of things lies open] (1:103).
"Mother" is the familiar name for the unfamiliar. It is an uncanny name for the Apollonian phenomenal world. Nietzsche describes it in terms very similar to those of Freud as the recognition
of the familiar in the unfamiliar: "Mit einem Erstaunen, das um so
grösser war, als sich ihm das Grausen beimischte, dass ihm jenes
alles doch eigentlich so fremd nicht sei, ja, dass sein apollinisches
Bewusstsein nur wie ein Schleier diese dionysische Welt vor ihm
verdecke" [With an amazement that was all the greater as it was
mingled with the horror that all this was actually not so foreign to
him, that only his Apollonian consciousness covered this Dionysian world as with a veil] (1:34). The uncanny evokes shudder
(*Schaudern*) in Faust and *Grausen* (horror, dread), even *Ekel* (nau-
sea), in Nietzsche. Nietzsche's language produces a link between
the phenomenalizing transformation of the maternal ground into
the visual world and the uncanny effect of shudder. Against
Schlegel's view of the chorus as the *idealische Zuschauer* (the ideal
spectator), Nietzsche calls him the "einzige *Schauer* . . ., der
Schauer der Visionswelt der Scene" [the only visionary, the visionary of the visionary world of the scene] (1:59). But the word
Schauer is also synonymous with *Schauder* (shudder). The pun
fuses the recall of the ancient phenomenal world with the effects
inspired by a revenant, the ghostly return of an image, a specter,
which Hölderlin already considered dangerous and which ends in
an explosion in Goethe's *Faust*.

Just as Freud sees Oedipus return as Hamlet in the modern
world, Nietzsche evokes Hamlet as the modern analogue to the
Dionysian man: "In diesem Sinne hat der dionysische Mensch Ähn-
lichkeit mit Hamlet: beide haben einmal einen wahren Blick in das
Wesen der Dinge getan, sie haben *erkannt,* und es ekelt sie zu han-
deln" [In this sense Dionysian man is similar to Hamlet: both have
had a true glance into the essence of things, they have *recognized,*
and it nauseates them to act] (1:56 ff.). This new Dionysian Ham-

let is closer to Socrates than to any Greek god. Freud called Hamlet a "secular progression in repression."[37] Nietzsche describes Socrates in terms of a radical shift in the function of negation: "Die instinctive Weisheit zeigt sich bei dieser gänzlich abnormen Natur nur, um dem bewussten Erkennen hier und da *hindernd* entgegenzutreten. Während doch bei allen productiven Menschen der Instinct gerade die schöpferisch-affirmative Kraft ist, und das Bewusstsein kritisch und abmahnend sich gebärdet: wird bei Sokrates der Instinct zum Kritiker, das Bewusstsein zum Schöpfer—eine wahre Monstrosität per defectum!" [The instinctual wisdom manifests itself in this completely abnormal nature only by countering conscious recognition through an inhibition. While in all productive human beings instinct is the creative-affirmative force and consciousness acts as an inhibition, the instinct becomes the critic, consciousness the creator in Socrates—a true monstrosity per defectum!] (1:90).

Only through this radical shift in the functions of repression, negation, eros, and death can Nietzsche recall the Greek gods, more precisely the duality of Dionysus and Apollo as they appear through the veiled mother in the eyes of Socrates and Hamlet.

3. Translations of Eros

Sophocles/Hölderlin
Baudelaire/Benjamin

The constellation of texts I discuss here—the third stasimon of the Sophoclean *Antigone* with Hölderlin's translation, and Baudelaire's "A une passante" with Benjamin's translation—might seem so arbitrary that even to call it a constellation needs to be questioned. The thematic link of Eros is brittle. What has the Eros invoked by the Sophoclean chorus to do with Baudelaire's precarious love poem of the modern big city (if we can call love poem this poem of an *amour manqué*, where love appears only in the remote impossibility of a past perfect subjunctive: *que j'eusse aimée*)?

It is the Eros of translation and the Eros in translation that brings them together here (as Eros is said to bring everything together) but also places and displaces them against each other (as Eros seems to do with everything). The Eros in translation raises the question of the translatability of Eros, the question whether "he" (whatever, whoever "he" is) can be transferred not only from one language into another but also from one culture and time into another, more specifically: from antiquity to modernity.

Eros, victorious in all battles and quarrels, as the Greek chorus addresses him (*erôs anikate machan* [v. 781], "Geist der Liebe, dennoch Sieger/Immer, in Streit!" [Spirit of love, yet victorious/ Always, in quarrel!], Hölderlin's translation, vv. 811 ff.): could he be victorious also in the *querelle des anciens et modernes*, victoriously asserting himself in the transfer and translation from one to the other? Freud, who did not hesitate to use ancient Greek models from Narcissus to Oedipus for his description and naming of modern erotic and sexual vicissitudes, nevertheless casts some doubt on the translatability of the ancient Eros. In a note, added in 1910 to his three treatises on sexual theory, Freud makes a rather sweeping statement about the difference of ancient and modern love: "The most incisive difference between the love life of the ancients and ours lies probably in the fact that antiquity placed the accent on the drive itself whereas we place it [*verlegen:* literally: shift, displace, mislay] on its object. The ancients celebrated the drive and were inclined to ennoble even an inferior object through the drive, whereas we value little the drive activity itself and excuse it only through the value of the object."[1]

If "we" have thus shifted, displaced, mislaid the accent of our love life, can we still speak of that Greek figure "Eros" in our loves? Or to phrase the question in another Freudian configuration of the historical vicissitudes of the drive: When the oedipal tragedy is translated into the melancholic drama of Hamlet, is Oedipus then still Oedipus as Hamlet? Has anything been translated, transferred in these transports of the heart and of desire? Anything?

Freud's note contains a German grammatical phrasing that is untranslatable in English: "daß die Antike den Akzent auf den Trieb selbst, wir aber auf dessen Objekt verlegen." German syntax makes it possible to use the verb *verlegen* only once at the end in relation to "us" (*wir . . . verlegen*) but implying it also for the first subject "antiquity." If the syntax implies the verb *verlegen* for antiquity, the accent has already been shifted, displaced, mislaid by the ancients. The English translation would thus have to make explicit what is implicit in German: "that antiquity shifts [or: shifted] the accent on the drive itself whereas we shift it on its object."

Eros, it seems, has already been shifted at the moment of his appearance. Eros perhaps is the shifter: free-floating mobility, the very condition for a mobile text, for the mobility from text to text and all the textual carryovers: translation, transfer, transport, metaphor. It might be noted, in passing, that transfer is the form of love in psychoanalysis.

From translation to translation we follow the ever roaming Sophoclean Eros, passing the night, through the night, and passing over the sea (*hos en malakaisi pareiais neanidos ennucheueis, phoitâs d'hyperpontios*) to the enigmatic *passante* of Baudelaire. The passage through these specific texts is motivated (as far as motivation can be grasped) by two determinate moments, one explicitly and emphatically inscribed in the relation of the translations, the other seemingly oddly accidental and coincidental.

The train of this motivation inverts the chronological line, beginning with the last of the texts: Benjamin's translation of Baudelaire's *Tableaux parisiens*. These translations were prefaced by the famous essay (which by now has almost completely overshadowed the translations themselves): "The Task of the Translator." This essay, as we have noted before, is not only permeated by echoes from Hölderlin, but it culminates in the evocation of Hölderlin's translations of Sophocles as the *Urbilder* (archetypal images) of true translation.[2] While an elaboration of this privileged position of Hölderlin's translation praxis in Benjamin's philosophy of translation would be a task in itself, it was an oddity in Benjamin's translation of "A une passante" and the coincidence of one word echoing between Benjamin and Hölderlin that led to this particular tracing of the translations of Eros.

At the crucial turn in Baudelaire's sonnet in the beginning of the tercets, after the night-producing lightning bolt—"Un éclair . . . puis la nuit"—beauty appears in the moment of its disappearance with the force of a life-giving power: "Fugitive beauté / Dont le regard m'a fait soudainement renaître" [Fugitive beauty, whose glance let me suddenly be reborn]. Benjamin renders these lines in a rather enigmatic turn of phrase: "Die Flüchtige, nicht leiht / Sie sich dem Werdenden an ihrem Schimmer" [The fugitive one, she does not lend herself to him, becoming (developing, growing) through (at) her shimmer].

The difficulty of rendering this phrase in English seems almost like an illustration of Benjamin's assertion that translations are untranslatable. It is, however, the specific German word *werden*, not only in its semantic complexities but also in the specific grammatical form in which it appears here, that makes a faithful, literal translation (but what is "faithful" and "literal" in translation?) so difficult. As the difficulty of a specific linguistic problem, it cannot be an illustration of the categorical untranslatability of translations claimed by Benjamin. The categorical untranslatability of translation means that we cannot, at any point, translate Benjamin's *translation* qua translation, even if the text of the translation poses no particular difficulties for translation. Translation, Benjamin says, is a "form," and it is the "form" of translation that is untranslatable.

Indeed, Benjamin explicitly says that it is not the difficulty (or gravity: *Schwere*) that makes translations untranslatable: "Übersetzungen dagegen erweisen sich unübersetzbar nicht wegen der Schwere, sondern wegen der allzu großen Flüchtigkeit, mit welcher der Sinn an ihnen haftet" [Translations, however, prove to be untranslatable not because of the gravity, but because of the all too great flightiness (fugitiveness) with which meaning adheres to them] (4:20). It is the fugitive meaning of translation ("wegen der allzu großen Flüchtigkeit, mit welcher der Sinn an ihnen haftet") that makes translations untranslatable in principle. Nevertheless, we have been guided to this categorical untranslatability at the moment when the translation of the *Fugitive beauté* and its/her effect on the poetic subject posed some specific difficulties for the retranslation into English. The problem clearly is not a problem of the untranslatability of translation, and yet it points in its specificity to that problem.

"Die Flüchtige, nicht leiht / Sie sich dem Werdenden an ihrem Schimmer": Fugitive beauty (or is it fugitive meaning? Benjamin erases the French *beauté*, leaves only a female fugitive) does not lend itself (or rather herself in the gendered German form) to him who yet becomes whatever he is only through her. And it is not even sure that we can talk of a "he" becoming, emerging here. Grammatically, *dem Werdenden* could be read as a neuter dative ("she does not lend herself to whatever is in the process of becoming"). Benjamin's translation not only blurs the French *beauté* to a mere shimmer but also the poetic subject being reborn into a depersonalized entity (a third "person" who is not a person) that is in the process of becoming. Fugitive beauty does not lend herself to that which is in the process of becoming, because as beauty it holds on, in all its fugitive evanescence, to the image of an unbroken Gestalt and form. It thus stands in contrast to the broken pieces of the language of translation and the language of the baroque of which Benjamin explicitly writes, that it lends itself: "Thus language is broken to pieces so that it can lend itself in its fragments to a transformed and intensified expression."[3]

What is in the process of becoming, *das Werdende,* in translation is, according to Benjamin's preface, pure language, even the kernel of pure language: "Es bleibt in aller Sprache und ihren Gebilden außer dem Mitteilbaren ein Nicht-Mitteilbares, ein, je nach dem Zusammenhang, in dem es angetroffen wird, Symbolisierendes oder Symbolisiertes. Symbolisierendes nur, in den endlichen Gebilden der Sprachen; Symbolisiertes aber im Werden der Sprache selbst. Und was im Werden der Sprachen sich darzustellen, ja herzustellen sucht, das ist jener Kern der reinen Sprache selbst" [There remains in all language and its forms something not communicable besides the communicable, something symbolizing or something symbolized, according to the context in which it is encountered. Symbolizing only in the finite forms of languages; but symbolized in the becoming (*Werden*) of language itself. What seeks to present, even to produce itself in the becoming of languages is that kernel of pure language itself] (4:19).

It seems, then, that Benjamin's translation is an allegory of the kernel of his philosophy of translation and language, and the allegorical figure of translation would be the figure of the erotic encounter: Eros as the figure of translation, but translation also as the figure of Eros.

But we must not hurry too fast to sweeping generalizations. Let us be guided by the words along their paths, their passes and impasses—especially their impasses, for it is at the moment of the impasse, when the word hits against impassable obstacles, that translation takes place—in the echo of the shattered word. Such, at least, is Hölderlin's poetic itinerary of the word:

> so kam
> Das Wort aus Osten zu uns,
> Und an Parnassos Felsen und am Kithäron hör' ich
> O Asia, das Echo von dir und es bricht sich
> Am Kapitol

[thus the word came to us from the East, and at the rocks of Parnassus and the Cithaeron I hear, O Asia, the echo from you, and it is refracted at the Capitol]. ("Am Quell der Donau," vv. 35–39)

The Greek mountains, the Roman hills, later the Alps are so many barriers; and there are no easy mountain passes for the word simply to cross: it breaks, shatters, refracts, and passes on in the echo. If, in Hölderlin's poetry, Asia is the name of the origin of the word, which can only be heard in the echo, Hölderlin's translations are for Benjamin the origin of translation, *Urbilder* of its form, resonating in fragmented echoes through his essay and translations. Through the echoes, something else is expected to be heard: the becoming of pure language in the transmissions and translations from language to language.

The curious appearance of a *Werdende* in Benjamin's translation of the effect of the erotic glance appears itself as an echo of a *Werden* in Hölderlin's translation of the apotheosis of desire through the eye of the beautiful young woman in the Sophoclean chorus:

Und nie zu Schanden wird es,
Das Mächtigbittende.
Am Augenliede der hochzeitlichen
Jungfrau, im Anbeginne dem Werden großer
Verständigungen gesellet. Unkriegerisch spielt nemlich
Die göttliche Schönheit mit

[And never comes to shame what is powerfully begging at the eyelid of the bridal young woman, associated in the beginning with the becoming of great understandings. Unwarlike namely divine beauty is in the play]. (FA 16:347–49, vv. 811–29)

Hölderlin's translation leads to the limit of understanding, to the threshold where understanding and sense are in the process of becoming and vanishing. Eros, love, desire seem closely linked to this threshold: "Sinnlos, doch lieb in liebem Tone sprichst du" [Senseless, but lovely in a loving tone you speak], says Ismene to Antigone in Hölderlin's translation (v. 101), acknowledging a "tone" in language beyond or before meaning and communication. And the tone is doubly linked to the word stem *lieb* (love).

2

In order to delineate more precisely this threshold, which is also the threshold of translation, the place of a transfer from language to language and of a transfer-love of a certain modernity and its becoming, in and through the transfer to Greek antiquity, we will have to explore more closely the texts on each side of the threshold and the echoes between them.

The Sophoclean invocation of Eros marks the transition between Haimon's angry departure after the quarrel with his father over Antigone's fate and the reappearance of Antigone on the way to her death. It seems directly related to the love between Haimon and Antigone, to which the chorus refers as the cause of the preceding quarrel between father and son: *sy kai tode neikos andrôn xynaimon echeis taraxas* [you (Eros) have also stirred up this quarrel between blood relatives] (vv. 794–95).[4]

Yet if there is passion and love between Haimon and Antigone, it is curiously understated in the play. Neither Haimon nor Antigone makes any passionate love declarations. In the quarrel between Kreon and Haimon, to which the chorus refers, Haimon argues less in the name of love than in the name of justice, reason—and in the name of his father, who, as father and ruler, is supposed to stand for justice and reason. Indeed, he begins with a gesture of complete submission: *pater, sos eimi* [Father, I am yours] (v. 637), and he continues saying that he will always follow his father, as long as he has useful and reasonable judgment (*gnômas echôn chrêstas*), and no marriage would be worth overstepping his father's good (more literally: beautiful) leadership (*sou kalôs hêgoumenou*). It is Kreon's obsession that his power might be threatened by a woman, and that only a woman could possibly turn his son away from complete obedience. It is he who suggests that Haimon only acts for the sake of the woman, whereupon Haimon emphatically corrects him: "*kai sou te, kai kamou, kai theôn nerterôn*" [and for your sake, and for mine, and for the sake of the gods of the underworld] (v. 751).

One might interject that Haimon's argument is mere strategy and that his threat and act of suicide in case of Antigone's death is the ultimate proof of his real passion for her. Yet the dialogue makes clear that Haimon is not afraid to confront his father radically if need be, and there is no reason to doubt the seriousness of the agencies he invokes, especially the last one: *kai theôn nerterôn*—the gods of the underworld. They, of course, are also the agencies invoked by Antigone. It will be in Antigone's tomb where he will be united with her—in death. If it is Eros that drives him there, it is a power that seems rather different from modern love tragedies. Haimon and Antigone are not Romeo and Juliet.

Antigone expresses even less than Haimon any specific attachment to her husband-to-be, or rather not-to-be. She laments her lot to die unwed ("agamos . . . erchomai"), to go to her tomb without wedding songs ("anymenaios"). Freud sensed something very essential when he remarked that the ancients put little investment in the object as such.

The celebration of Eros and his power by the chorus literally takes the place of the encounter between Haimon and Antigone that never takes place. Kreon wants Antigone to be brought before Haimon's eyes, to die in his presence ("*hôs kat' ommat' autika / paronti thnêskê,*" v. 763). Haimon violently refuses and disappears, promising that also he, Kreon, would never see him again "with his eyes" [en ophthalmois horôn]. We will have to come back to this emphasis on seeing and the eye. Haimon disappears, avoiding the appearance of Antigone in order to encounter her only as a corpse in the tomb. He himself will return to the stage at the end as a corpse in his father's arms.

If there are love declarations in *Antigone,* they are all directed at corpses: Kreon's love for his son and child now as a corpse in his arms; Haimon's love for Antigone fulfilled in a bloody wedding to the hanging corpse in the tomb; and, from the beginning, the most intense love declaration expressed by Antigone for the dead brother with whom she anticipates to lie in love forever, as the Greek text in its repetition of *philos* suggests: "philê met'autou keisomai, philou meta" (v. 73). Hölderlin's translation reproduces the intensity and the erotic connotation of "lying with" (the position of the "meta" [with] at the end of the verse gives it special emphasis) the loved/lovely brother: "Lieb werd' ich bei ihm liegen, bei dem Lieben" [Loved/loving I will lie with him the loved/loving one] (the predicate *lieb* in German has the connotation both of being loved, someone who is "dear," and one who gives love).

Charles Segal points out a curious correlation between the motive of the corpse and the contemporary Greek discovery of the beautiful body in sculpture: "Sophocles presents a play that centers about the desecration of a human body at the very time that his contemporaries working on the Parthenon were discovering and expressing the beauty and nobility of man's body as it had never been expressed before."[5] What Segal calls "the beauty and nobility of man's body" is at the center of the occidental ideal of the imagination and its specular investment in Greek antiquity. The classical ideal of Greek sculpture as expression of the human body as totalizing Gestalt went hand in hand with an intense interest in anatomy and dissection. Could it be, then, that the image of the beautiful whole body is born from the decomposition and dismemberment of the corpse? Or perhaps, more precisely, is it the Fata Morgana of a mirror image emerging from the corpse, as the image of Antigone suddenly appears to the guards after a blinding sandstorm near the corpse of Polyneikes? The translation of the stinking, rotting corpse into the beautiful image of the erotic body is mediated through a moment of blindness which the guard calls "theyan noson" [a divine illness] (v. 423) and which Hölderlin translates as "göttlich Weh": divine suffering. In his notes on *Antigone*, Hölderlin ascribes to the chorus parts the function of "suffering organs of the divine struggling body" [als *leidende Organe* des göttlichringenden Körpers] (FA 16:419). They accompany the more violent and inexorable dialogues "haltend oder deutend" [restraining or interpreting]. They translate (but like all translation also stop, interrupt, bring to a halt, and support: *haltend*) something that transgresses all forms (and thus the image of all forms: the body) and understanding into understandable form (*verständlich gefaßt*). They are human understanding and reason walking in the midst of the unthinkable ("des Menschen Verstand, als unter Undenkbarem wandelnd," FA 16:413).

If we follow Hölderlin's perspective of the chorus, we must read the chorus to Eros as a translation of "Eros," that is, a translation of "something" unthinkable into some understandable form, which seems indeed the resume of the tragedy, when the chorus sums up its reflections: "Pollô to phronein eudaimonias/Prôton hyparchei" —in Hölderlin's translation: "Um vieles ist das Denken mehr, denn Glükseligkeit" [By much thinking is more, than happiness]. But there would be no thinking without the unthinkable of the tragic pain and blissfulness that it translates.

3

Let us begin, then, belatedly, with a reading and thinking of the first translation of Eros, as the Greek chorus translates the unthinkable into its language and form.

From the outset, Eros is placed emphatically in the context of battle, quarrel, and competition. The first line addresses him as "unconquered in battle" [*anikate machan*]. His victoriousness is carried over to his associates: desire ("nikâ . . . himeros") and Aphrodite ("amachos . . . theos Aphrodita"). The second line repeats the invocation of the name and gives it an aggressive twist: "erôs hos en ktêmasi pipteis" [Eros, who falls upon, who attacks wealth and possessions]—*empiptein* has a strong military connotation of an army intruding a country.[6] Not only is Eros victoriously involved in battles and aggressions, but he is even the cause of war and quarrel, and specifically of the one going on in this particular case: "sy kai tode neikos andrôn xynaimos echeis taraxas" [You also have stirred up this quarrel between men who are blood relatives]. It is generally and reasonably assumed that this refers to the preceding quarrel between Haimon and Kreon. But the reference to the quarrel of blood relatives might also include the original battle between the brothers that is the ground of this tragedy. One might even hear in the Greek *neikos* and *xynaimos* the echo of both names: Poly*neikes*, the unburied dead brother, and H*aimon*, Kreon's son and Antigone's fiancé. Antigone is linked with both by ties of love. While the causality of Eros in the brotherly war might be enigmatic, it is nevertheless striking that the second address to

Eros describes him in the very act that made Polyneikes an outcast in the eyes of Kreon: *hos en ktêmasi pipteis*, the one who attacks, falls upon, intrudes into the possessions of another.

Hölderlin translates the name Eros first as *Geist der Liebe* (spirit of love) and in the second line as *Friedensgeist* (spirit of peace), which contrasts him to Ares as *Schlachtgeist* (spirit of battle), as Hölderlin translates the name Ares in verse 144. The opposition of Eros and Ares, of *Friedensgeist* and *Schlachtgeist*, is, however, blurred through the presentation of Eros in terms of battle and discord. But this blurring points at the core of Hölderlin's poetics of tragedy as the presentation of highest unity through the most intense discord and oppositions.

This might suggest a dialectical reading as it has become most famous through Hegel's interpretation. Leaving aside for the moment the particular ethical forces at stake in Hegel's reading, we may notice a great deal of support in the Sophoclean text for the more general Hölderlinian formula of tragedy as a presentation of unity through discord and splitting. The very first verse of the play draws the figure of such a dialectic of unity and splitting when Antigone addresses Ismene: "Ô koinon autadelphon Ismênês kara" (in Hölderlin's translation: "Gemeinsamschwesterliches! o Ismenes Haupt" [O common sisterly, O Ismene's head]). The double emphasis on unity and oneness in the Greek *koinon autadelphon* is countered by the decapitation that makes Ismene's head the metonymic representative of the addressed person. Although this particular metonymy is rather common in the Sophoclean plays,[7] it nevertheless gains specific rhetorical force in the contrast with the semantic emphasis on unity.

The movement of the dialogue performs the splitting: what begins with the invocation of closest unity ends in a radical separation. This movement is repeated in the dialogue between Haimon and Kreon, which begins with a declaration of unity (*"pater, sos eimi"*) and ends not only with Haimon's leaving in anger, but again also with the metonymic separation of his head: "sy t'oudamâ / toumon prosopsei krât' en ophthalmois horôn" [never will you see with your eyes my head again].

The two brothers who died on one day from two hands (which were each other's brotherly hands) and leave the two sisters united in the common loss to be separated again in hate and misunderstanding drives the Sophoclean language into a virtuoso act of the Greek dualis: "dyoin adelphoin esterêthêmen dyo,/miâ thanontôn hêmera diplê cheri" (in Hölderlin's translation: "seitdem/Die beiden Brüder beide wir verloren; Die starben, Einen Tag, von zweien Händen") [Since both brothers we both lost; they died, on One day from two hands]. Tiresias, the blind seer, introduces himself and his guide as "dy' ex henos bleponte" [two seeing out of one] (v. 986).

But most of all it is in the sphere of Eros and love where the separations tear most violently into the unities. Antigone, who claims to be here to love and not to hate, is yet inexorable in the expression of her hatred when Ismene does not immediately go along with her. Hölderlin underlines the interchangeability of Eros and Ares when he translates in the parodos the *"pyrphoros"* (fire carrying), characterizing Ares acting through Polyneikes as "Liebestrunken" (drunken with love). Ares and Eros merge here under the sign of Dionysus/Bacchus, who is the one with the many names and for Hölderlin also the creator of names.

That which brings Eros and Ares together under the sign of Dionysus, and infuses a fundamental ambivalence into Eros as love and hatred, is the common effect of a terrifying violence that shakes and shatters any given order and identity: *Erschüttern* in Hölderlin's vocabulary. The Greek text first ascribes this effect to Ares in the parodos (vv. 141–43): "ta men alla, tad' ep' allois epenôma styphelizôn megas Arês dexioseiros" [Shaking things up, the great Ares, like the strong horse to the right, distributes some things this way, others to others]. Hölderlin's translation emphasizes even more the violent seismic effect through an elaboration of the metaphor of the leading, stronger horse to the right (*dexioseiros*): "Anderes andrem/Bescheidet der Schlachtgeist, wenn der hart/ Anregend einen mit dem Rechten die Hand erschüttert" [Other things to others distributes distinctly the battle spirit when he, hard stirring, shakes up one's hand with the right]. In the word *Beschei-*

det Hölderlin contracts the act of separation (*scheiden*) and (re-) distribution. *Erschüttern* (shaking things up, destruction) is for Hölderlin the ground for Gestalt (form, shape, construction). There is no such thing as reconstruction.

As the one who redistributes things through shattering the given order, creating new right, as Hölderlin's translation of *dexioseiros* suggests, Ares appears as the force of the Moira, that ultimate, irreducible Greek principle of distribution. It is related to the word *meros* (part, share, portion, role, rank), which, in Plato's *Phaidros*, enters into a close association with Eros through the mediation of *himeros* (desire, charm) and its etymological relation (according to Socrates) to *meros:* "Hotan men oun blepousa pros to tou paidos kallos, ekeithen merê epionta kai reont' (ha dê tauta himeros kaleitai)" (251c).[8]

In the Sophoclean text Ares and Eros are linked partly directly, partly through Dionysus/Bacchus to Eros. The stirring and shattering (*styphelizôn*) of Ares corresponds to the almost synonymous *elelizôn* of the Bacchus dance a few lines later (v. 157). And Eros "himself" is characterized in the word *taraxas* (v. 795: one who stirs things up, disarranges, dishevels—in Hölderlin's strong translation: "wirfst es untereinander" [throw it in disarray]).

In this activity of shaking things up, throwing them in disarray, Eros seems to function like the "nurse of becoming" [*geneseôs tithênên*] in Plato's *Timaeus* (52d), who, shaking and being shaken, prepares the order of the world, separating the dissimilar and bringing together the similar. Yet there is also a striking difference: the Eros of the Sophoclean chorus enters into an already ordered and established world and shakes it up: he "falls upon" already established orders of property (*en ktêmasi pipteis*), he roams not only over the sea (*phoitâs d'hyperpontios*), but also intrudes into the cultured land and settlements (*en t'agronomois aulais*); and above all he threatens established right and laws through a subversive complicity with the unlawful, trespassing side of the minds of the righteous: "sy kai dikaiôn adikous phrenas paraspâs epi lôba" [you lead astray into shame also the unjust minds of the just]. Eros is addressed as an agency of transgression. And yet there is

also a suggestion of an intricate complicity with the very foundation of law in the enigmatic (and by some disputed) lines: "tôn
megalôn paredros en archais thesmôn" [table companion in the
government (or: in the beginning) of the great laws]. However, this
table companion (*paredros*) is no longer strictly speaking Eros,
because Eros "himself" has undergone a double transformation
and translation. Instead of the victorious Eros (*erôs anikate machan*) appears now *himeros* (desire, longing, charm) as the victor
(*nikâ . . . himeros*), followed or accompanied by the equally victorious but also unwarlike female god and figure of Aphrodite: *amachos gar empaizei theos Aphrodita*. These transfigurations of Eros
are presented in a transformation of the discourse: the address and
apostrophe to Eros changes into a third-person narrative at the
moment when *himeros* appears. The change is marked by the transformation of the vocative *anikate* to the third-person verb form:
nikâ.

This transformation seems intimately linked to the figure of appearance itself. Victorious *himeros,* namely, is emphatically victorious through apparition, connected with the eye: "nikâ d'enargês
blepharôn himeros eulektrou nymphas" [victorious is the visible
(manifest, apparent, shining) desire of the eyelids of the charming
(well-bedded, good in bed, sexy) young woman]. The figure of the
prosopopoeia conjures into allegorical presence the invisible agency
of Eros. When Eros appears visibly in the figure *himeros* in and
through the eye, or rather, when the eyelid of the eroticized woman
is read as a visible sign of Eros, a narrative, descriptive, and reflex-
ive mode replaces the apostrophe, on which it yet depends.

The metonymic representation of the eye and its phenomenol-
ogy through the *blepharon,* the eyelid or eyelash, brings into focus,
with the batting of an eye, the matrix and structure of erotic significance as an organizing force of this text. The naked eye has no
erotic appeal; it gains it only through its occasional occlusion and
veiling by the eyelid, the batting of the eye. It is the condition of
the glance of the eye, which in turn is the condition for the erotic
moment. It produces the glance of the eye, the *Augenblick* and its
temporality as the momentous moment. Without the eyelid, the eye

becomes monstrous, and seeing vanishes into the monstrosity of the limitless nonimage as Kleist evokes it before a seascape of Caspar David Friedrich: "The image lies there with its two or three mysterious objects like the apocalypse, as if it had Young's night thoughts, and because it has, in its monotony and limitlessness, nothing but the frame as a foreground, it is, when one looks at it, as if one's eyelids were cut off."[9] Eyelidless eye and limitless, shoreless (*uferlos*) image merge together in the apocalypse, which is literally revelation, but as revelation in the extreme and without boundaries, it is also the revelation of catastrophe in a catastrophe of revelation.

If, according to chaos theory, the batting of the wing of a butterfly can be the origin of apocalyptic hurricanes, the batting of the eyelid seems to reveal the eye of a textual hurricane generating the tragic text.

The first large chorus part, the parodos of the Sophoclean *Antigone*, begins with an invocation of the sun and the revelation of light: "aktis aelioio, to kalliston heptapylô phanen Thêbâ tôn proterôn phaos" [O beam of the sun, most beautiful light of the ancestors that appeared to the seven gates of Thebes]. What once appeared appears now again: "ephanthês pot' ô chryseas hameras blepharon" [finally you have revealed yourself again, O eyelid of the golden day].

Hölderlin translates the *aktis aelioio* as "O Blik der Sonne: [O glance of the sun], and the *blepharon* as "O Augenblik des goldenen Tages" [O moment (eye glance) of the golden day]. In eighteenth-century German and still in Hölderlin's vocabulary *Blick* (glance) and *Blitz* (lightning bolt) are interchangeable: the momentous moment of revelation—"un éclair . . . puis la nuit." Hölderlin's commentary interprets tragedy precisely as such a moment: "The boldest moment of the course of a day or of a work of art is when the spirit of time and nature, the heavenly power that seizes man, and the object in which he is interested stand most ferociously against each other, because the sensuous object extends only halfway, but the spirit wakes up most powerfully where the second half begins. In this moment, man must hold fast most, therefore he stands there most openly in his character."[10] It is the moment of an apocalypse as a revelation in the moment of a catastrophical rupture between the phenomenological and spiritual world, between sense and the senses. It is the moment of a translation in the breakdown of translation.

With the batting of an eye: there is light and then darkness, there is day and then night. The parodos that begins with the greeting of the light and the apparent victory moves through the recapitulation of the ferocious battle to an invitation to all-night Dionysian feasts: *chorois pannychois* (v. 155). These all-night Dionysian feasts are echoed in the third stasimon by the invocation of Eros, who passes the night on the soft cheeks of the young woman: "hos en malakaisi pareiais neanidos ennycheueis." He is, essentially, the one who passes the night, passes through the night, *übernachtet* in Hölderlin's translation, translating, as Bernhard Böschenstein remarked, translation itself: that crossing over from precarious sense to precarious sense through the nightly *mise en abîme* of sense between the languages.[11] While he spares neither immortals nor mortals, he seems to have a special relation to the latter, who are called *hameriôn* (belonging to the day, ephemeral). As such they are the other half of the nightly god, but like him transient in essence, or rather, in continuous oscillation between light and darkness, day and night. Texts are the frozen moments of this oscillation.

Eros, having passed the night on the cheek of the young woman, wakes up with her, on her eyelid, enters into the visible world as *himeros,* as desire speaking from and through the blinking of her eye. The Greek text calls this also the play of Aphrodite, which Hölderlin reads and translates as "divine beauty."

The translation of Eros into manifest appearance would seem also a translation from male to female. This is surprising both in the context of Greek culture, where the woman is generally relegated to the private and secret world of the hearth, and in the specific context of the Sophoclean tragedy, where Antigone is the guardian and spokeswoman of the secret world of the dead, the underworld, and the family in opposition to Kreon's public world of the day.

Indeed, the sexual and textual relations are not that simple. Eros appears as *himeros* (a masculine noun) through the eye(lid) of the beautiful woman, hovering in the ambivalent grammatical position of a subjective and objective genitive: as desire of her eyes and for her eyes. The female divinity Aphrodite is somehow 'in the play' (*empaizei*), playing along 'in' it. When Hölderlin translates Aphrodite as divine beauty, he places her precisely on the threshold of the manifest phenomenological world: for beauty is both manifestation and veiling through appearance. Beauty is the invisible in the visible.

If Aphrodite is in the play as divine beauty, it is Antigone who embodies beauty and the dialectics of eros in the human world. She is the *blepharon* for the creatures of the day: coming from darkness and going into darkness, the blinking of an eye. Wherever she appears to them, it is as a stunning and threatening apparition. As an apparition, Antigone is not 'nature' (with which a conventional rhetoric tends to associate woman) but a figure of art, not only in the narrow sense of the work of art (to which Adorno ascribes "apparition" as an essential quality)[12] but in the wider sense of the human world and civilization that owes its specificity—the erotic, language, the rites for the dead—to a symbolic order.

Kreon has a paranoic fear that there might be anything not transparent. Not to be able to penetrate soul, thought, and opinion of every man ("pantos andros ekmathein psychên te, kai phronêma, kai gnômên," v. 179) shakes the ground of power. The worst thing for Kreon is a "closed tongue" [glôssan egkleisas echei kakistos] (vv. 183 ff.). The gravity of silence (*sigês baros*), when Kreon's wife silently withdraws into her house and death, will later mark the turning moment when Kreon reappears on stage with a scream: *iô*.

In this world of patent power, Antigone appears as pure cryptic enigma. *Kryptein* (*kata chthonos ekrypse*, vv. 24 ff.) and *kalyptein* (*taphô kalypsai*, v. 28)—"hiding," "making secret," "covering up," "veiling"—are also the words used for burying the dead and thus describe Antigone's transgressive and ultimately revealing, apocalyptic act. When Kreon first hears of this act and asks who did it, the guard answers, "ouk oid'" [I don't know]. Hölderlin translates, however, "Undenklich" [Unthinkable]. The translation thus does not read simple, circumstantial ignorance but indicates a structural impossibility. (Even in everyday life, the expression "I don't know" often stands for something that the subject cannot and does not want to think, something unthinkable.) Hölderlin translates the words of a tragic/comic, fearful, and not all too brilliant guard as a symptom of that *Verstand, als unter Undenkbarem wandelnd* (reason [understanding] walking under [in the midst of] the unthinkable). A traceless actor (*asêmos hourgatês*) of the night has committed an act that appears to the glance of the day (*hêmeroskopos;* Hölderlin translates: "Tagesblik") as a miracle (*thauma*).

Antigone repeats her act, this time in broad daylight, or rather, in the blinking of daylight. The sun has reached the middle of the sky and seems to stand still for a moment, which for the Greeks was also the moment of Pan, a panic moment of ominous silence. Hölderlin's translation brings this panic into the focus of a cosmic catastrophe: "bis auseinander brechend / Der Sonne Kreis sich bükte grad herab" [until, breaking apart, the sun's circle bent down straight]. At this moment of high noon a blinding sandstorm rises, covering the scene and causing the guards to cover themselves in their "divine suffering" [theian noson]. The blinking of an eye: they open their eyes, and now they see—a child with the sharp, shrill voice of a bird (*hê pais horâtai*). Antigone's apparition out of the blinding moment is presented in a curious mixture of an appeasing familiarity (*hê pais*) and disconcerting strangeness (*ornythos oxyn pthoggon*). (For the Greeks, who called all non-Greeks *barbaroi,* all foreign languages sounded like the twirping of birds.)[13]

When the chorus, just after having asserted to stay clear from anyone transgressing the laws, sees her entering with the guard as his prisoner, she appears to them as a "demonic sign," or even a monster (*es daimonion teras*). Hölderlin again translates strongly: "Wie Gottesversuchung aber stehet es vor mir" [Like divine temptation it stands before me]. Antigone has something profoundly unsettling for the reasonable translators of the unthinkable. That becomes clear when they see her again on her way to her tomb as the apparition that emerges from their invocation of Eros, or perhaps irrupts in it. The song and dance of the chorus gives its due to the power of desire but secures it somewhat in its association with the beginnings and rules of the law: *paredros en archais thesmôn*. But when the chorus actually sees (*tad' horôn*) the apparition of desire in Antigone, its song and dance gets carried away, gets out of tune, and step, and law: "nyn d'êdê 'gô kautos thesmôn exô pheromai tad' horôn" [But now, even I myself am carried outside of the law, seeing this]. Hölderlin's translation breaks up the syntax, setting off almost each word by itself through commas and line break: "Jezt aber komm' ich, eben, selber, aus/Dem Geseze." But what is "this" that the chorus sees? It is not just a beautiful woman batting her eyes. It is the blinking of the eye itself in Antigone's passing through a moment of apocalyptic, revealing light into the darkness of Eros and death: "hoth' horô thalamon tên d'Antigonên anytousan" [since I see this Antigone going her path to the end into the bridal chamber]. She is literally *une passante* that makes the chorus cringe.

4

Our reading of the Greek text already took recourse from time to time to Hölderlin's translation. The fiction of a pure Greek text before the translation could not be sustained, once the effect of this translation had placed it before the "original." The reading could only attempt to trace its own performance in the passing between the texts, hovering over the waters, as Hölderlin translates *d'hyperpontios*.

Nevertheless, it is time now to focus more precisely on the transfers of the translation, or at least on some aspects of it. We might begin with the "trans-" itself, which in German usually appears as *über* (*Übersetzung, Übertragung*) and which Hölderlin's *Übersetzung* marks emphatically as the position of Eros: "Friedensgeist, der *über*/Gewerb einniket, und *über* zärtlicher Wange bei/Der Jungfrau *über*nachtet,/Und schwebet *über* Wassern" [Spirit of peace that falls asleep over business and that passes the night ("overnights") over the tender cheek with the young woman, and hovers over the waters]. *Über* corresponds most closely to the English "over": hovering over, crossing over, passing over, over something, or perhaps over nothing, over a gap, over an abyss. Falling asleep over such trivialities as business and trade (*Gewerb*) would be the lover's ironic judgment of such things: the seemingly less aggressive translation of *en ktêmasi pipteis* only annihilates them all the more effectively as boring trivia.

Eros is over and above all and nothing, and above all he marks a relation, he is a pre-position, which affects all relations and prepositions. The Greek text sums up his transgressive passings and passions in one short phrase: "ho d'echôn memênen" [whoever has it/him, is mad]. This becomes in Hölderlin's translation a disturbing confounding and displacement of prepositional relations: "und es ist / Wer's an sich hat, nicht bei sich" [and whoever has it on him is not by (with) himself]. Eros "himself," who has been addressed so far in the figure of apostrophe, becomes in Hölderlin's translation an 's, an *apostrophe s*. The *O* that is in many languages the letter of apostrophe (*Antigone* begins with it: ô *koinon autadelphon . . .*) has itself become an apostrophe in this "[W]er's."

Eros has inserted his apostrophe into the one who has him, and has split him from himself. The German prepositions *an* and *bei* both indicate immediate proximity (at, with) and are sometimes interchangeable.[14] But *bei* has the specific connotation of being at home with someone, being in the sphere of someone's being and dwelling. According to Grimm's *Deutsches Wörterbuch*, it is etymologically related to *bau* and *bauen* (build, building), in this respect analogous to the French *chez*, which some etymologists derive from *casa*, but also to "being," which in German appears in the first person singular as *bin*.

Eros is thus the one who unsettles the very being of the subject, dislocating it from itself, from its dwelling, from its being. Eros is here revealed as the source of a phenomenon invoked in the first and second stasimon: human existence as driving out or being driven out from its dwelling. In the first stasimon the chorus presents this dislocation in the image of the sails as wings that carry the ships out over the sea. Hölderlin translates (perhaps through a

misunderstanding of the Greek *oidmasin*): "fähret er aus / In geflü-
gelten sausenden Häußern" [he drives out in winged, whizzing
houses]. But his translation also recalls Plato's *Phaidros*, according
to which the true, divine name of Eros is Pteros, the winged one
(*thnêtoi men Erôta kalousi potênon, athanatoi de Pterôta*, 252b).
In Plato, the translation of the mortal name of Eros into the immortal name of Pteros is also the moment of another carryover: the
transport of the senses into another sense, the event of the metaphor.
This event reaches a climax a little later in the name of *himeros* as
the god-given name for an orgiastic exchange and transfer of liquids, where the stability of literal and metaphorical sense is utterly
liquidated: "then, touching each other in the gymnasia and other
places, the source of that flow that Zeus called *himeros* when he
loved Ganymed [*hon himeron Zeus Ganymêdos erôn ônomasen*],
flows richly toward the lover, partly flowing into him, partly flowing out of him who has been filled up" (255c). Eros/Himeros gives
wings to the words for an infinite transport.

Such transports shatter any dwelling and house. One of the
effects of this shattering is, according to the second stasimon, *Atê*,
a kind of fatal blindness, miscognition, and general misfortune:
"an seithê theothen domos, atas ouden elleipei" [when a house is
shaken up from the side of the god, *atê* will not be lacking] (vv.
584 ff.). Hölderlin translates: "wenn sich reget von Himmlis-
chen / Einmal ein Haus, fehlts dem an Wahnsinn nicht" [if once a
house is stirred by the heavenly ones, madness will not be lacking].
The translation names here already the madness proclaimed in the
third stasimon as the effect of Eros and appears there as the transfer and transport itself in a radical split of oneself from oneself.

Eros does not remain "himself"; he is translated into *er's* and
into an *es* of pure desire that keeps powerfully begging: "Und nie
zu Schanden wird es, / Das Mächtigbittende." And it is not, it 'becomes': "wird es." *Werden* is the great competitor of *Sein* in German. Its linguistic, rhetorical, and ideological history would have
to be an essential part of any analysis of German history. Hölderlin's translation inscribes it in an overdetermined constellation of
relations and associations. The word *Werden* is, at this point, not

a translation but an inscription into the translation: "im Anbeginne [*en archais*] dem Werden [————] großer [*megalôn*] Verständigungen [*thesmôn*] gesellet [*paredros*]." Each Greek word has its translation (boldly interpreted sometimes, as the *Verständigungen* for *thesmôn*), but there is no Greek word corresponding to the *Werden.*

Hölderlin translates the *en archais* as if it were the *en archê* of the gospel of John: in the beginning. In the beginning, according to John, was the logos, the word, as it is usually translated, although some translators, among them Goethe's Faust, had problems with this translation. Hölderlin seems at least to hint at the logos with his translation of *thesmôn* (position, what has been posited, law) as *Verständigungen* (understanding, communication), or rather as the "becoming of understanding and communication." If a position, a topos, a law is the pre-position of any understanding, it is yet, in Hölderlin's translation, a positioning in constant flow and liquidity. Precisely because Eros and desire are in the beginning associated with the becoming of communication, every posited sense, every thetic act, is already carried away and displaced, in the beginning, by the transports and metaphors of the erotic tongue. *Im Anbeginne*, writes Hölderlin, and recalls with the *an* that precedes the beginning that he who has it *an sich* is not *bei sich.* Being *im Anbeginne* is already no longer being with itself, already split from any beginning, the accent has already been shifted: *verlegt* by this mobile shifter Eros.

For Eros hovers over waters: "schwebet über Wassern," recalling another beginning, the *bereshet* of the Hebrew bible: "in the beginning," or as Chouraqui's beautifully literal French translation gives it: *entête*, marking the relation to the word *rosh* ("head"). *Antigone,* we remember, begins with an apostrophe to a head: ô *koinon autadelphon Ismênês kara,* opening a dialogue that ends in complete misunderstanding. Should we understand that misunderstanding stands at the beginning of the becoming of great understandings? Perhaps yes, since Eros after all (and before all) is the great disturber of understandings, the one who stirs up trouble and quarrel even between those who are supposed to be in natural understanding. After all (and before all) Eros is a highly unnatural force: breaking up the "natural" family ties, not just occasionally, but in principle according to the elementary structures that govern the social and sexual exchanges of the human animal at the threshold of "nature" and "culture."

Hölderlin's translation posits Eros as spirit (*Geist*) over the waters in the position of the Elohim and his/their breath hovering over the waters (the little breath of an *h* before the over makes it hover). In this position, he becomes identical (but is there still identity, where Eros is?) with the creative word itself, for this spirit creates by speaking, as pure performative word. And the creative word in German, since Luther's translation of the Bible, is: *Es werde.* In becoming "identical" with this creative word, Eros loses all identity, shifts from position to position, from the Elohim to Dionysus who, in Hölderlin's translation, is addressed as "Nahmenschöpfer, der du von den Wassern, welche Kadmos / Geliebet, der Stolz bist" [Creator of names, you who are the pride of the waters that Kadmos loved] (vv. 1162 ff.). But who is Dionysus? Part of an echo: "deß, der im Echo donnert, / Ein Theil, des Vaters der Erd'" [of him, who thunders in the echo, a part, of the father of the earth]. As an echo of an echo, as a translation of translation, Eros is yet posited before and over all this flow and liquids— before and over: *vor* and *über—vorüber,* passing by, passed, *passant, passé.*

He passes in a particular way: with the blinking of an eye, in an *Augenblick.* Faust's desperate search for an alternative translation of logos finds a rather unique addition in Hölderlin's translation of the last words of the chorus in *Antigone,* when the "great words" [*megaloi de logoi*] (v. 1340) are given as "Große Blike aber" [great glances]. They, according to Hölderlin's translation, "have taught us to think, in old age": "Sie haben im Alter gelehrt, zu denken."

5

Hölderlin's poem "Bread and Wine," which traces the detours of transubstantiation, the emergence of the sign in the consumption of the world, begins with nightfall and the noise of carriages and coaches rushing away: "Ringsum ruhet die Stadt; still wird die erleuchtete Gasse, / Und, mit Fakeln geschmükt, rauschen die Wagen hinweg" [All around the city rests; the illuminated streets become silent, and the carriages, adorned with torches, rush away]. The amorphous noise of *rauschen* also invokes the word *Rausch,* intoxication as the dissolution of the established perception and transformation into another order. Half a century later, in the "capital of the 19th century," the scene has changed. No longer the magic of illuminated carriages rushing away, giving room to rest and silence, but deafening noise surrounds the "moi": "La rue assourdissante autour de moi hurlait."

The deafening, dulling of the senses becomes the scene of an apparition. A line, an outline, a silhouette of beauty emerges from the cacophony: "Longue, mince." The figure is in mourning: "en grand deuil." Being in mourning is not necessarily the same as being sad; indeed, it does not necessarily describe any "inner" state. It is at least as much a display of mourning at the specific occasion of death: "*deuil:* Douleur, affliction que l'on eprouve de la mort de quqn.; Mort d'un proche; Signes extérieurs du deuil, consacrés par l'usage. Vêtements de deuil (noir, dans notre civilisation)," according to Robert. Benjamin's translation underlines the visual display of mourning, adding it, without comma, to the drawing of the lines of the figure: "Hoch schlank tiefschwarz." Apparitions and literary figures have no emotions, but they can figure them: "douleur majestueuse," signified in the signs of being "en grand deuil." Being "en grand deuil" means first of all being able to wear the appropriate clothes and knowing how to wear them with the appropriate "allure." Uncontrolled expression of sadness and loss would undo the very state of being "en grand deuil." There is, of course, always the temptation, deeply ingrained through a long tradition of psychologizing sentimentality, to discredit the display of mourning as mere show in favor of genuine inner feelings. It will find a powerful, eloquent voice at the threshold of modernity in Hamlet's protestations of true mourning:

Seems, madam? Nay, it is. I know not "seems."
'Tis not alone my inky cloak, good mother,
Nor customary suits of solemn black,
Nor windy suspiration of forc'd breath,
No, nor the fruitful river in the eye,
Nor the dejected haviour of the visage,
Together with all forms, moods, shapes of grief,
That can denote me truly. These indeed seem,
For they are actions that a man might play;
But I have that within which passes show,
These but the trappings and the suits of woe. (I, 2, 76–86)

But even Hamlet will have to acknowledge the force and power of playacting when he hears the actor recite Hecuba's woes, and he begins to wonder about his seemingly true "motive" and "cue for passion" (II, 2, 545 ff.). Hamlet became one of the most favorite figures of theatrical display and posturing, particularly in the nineteenth century. Baudelaire's favorite painter, Delacroix, caught some of these postures and gestures of morbid melancholia in his paintings. Melancholia is essentially theatrical, as Benjamin portrays it in his book on the German baroque drama. And there is a great deal of theatrical posturing and gesticulation in Baudelaire's self-presentation.

Only in the third line is the figure of the "douleur majestueuse" revealed as a woman, who knows how to handle her clothes ("d'une main fasteuse") and control her gait ("agile et noble"). She handles her appearance with a balancing act of the seam of her dress, balancing the borderline between the seemly and unseemly,[15] between the visible and the invisible.

Veiled and revealed at the same time is the metonymic object of desire: "sa jambe de statue." More precisely, an artifact has been produced in the space between the visible and the invisible in the border zone of the phenomenal, in the transport and metaphor of the senses where the beautiful is (dis-)located with and through the ever mobile, agile Eros. In Georg Büchner's novella *Lenz*, the poet passionately argues against an idealizing art in favor of a mimesis of life and nature, for the "feeling that whatever is created be full of life." But then he illustrates this desire with a curious image. He recalls a scene from one of his walks, where he saw two young women sitting on a stone. One helps the other tying up her hair. One of them seems in mourning: "a serious pale face, and yet so young, and her black costume." Lenz is enthralled by the image and wishes to capture it: "Sometimes one would like to be a Medusa head in order to transform such a group into stone." The desire for life in art becomes the desire for petrification in order to freeze and eternalize the passing beauty. And yet it is precisely its passing through the twilight of the phenomenal that produces the effect of the beautiful.

Antigone, the stunning apparition of a desire that is located at the origin of the laws (*en archais thesmôn*) and threatens to dislocate the translating chorus outside the laws (*thesmôn exô*), compares and identifies herself with Niobe turned to stone, a moment when Hölderlin's translation outdoes itself in eery beauty:

Ich habe gehört, der Wüste gleich sei worden
Die Lebenreiche, Phrygische,
Von Tantalos im Schoose gezeugt, an Sipylos' Gipfel;
Hökricht sei worden die und wie eins Epheuketten
Anthut, in langsamen Fels
Zusammengezogen

[I have heard, that she became like the desert, the one full of life, the Phrygian woman, begotten by Tantalus in the womb, near the summit of Sipylos, that she became hunchbacked and, as someone puts on ivy, contracted into slow rock]. (vv. 852–57)

Baudelaire's poem performs its own petrification of the passing, agile, sexy flesh into the "jambe de statue." Benjamin's translation catches this contraction of agility and petrification in a "Knie gegossen": the cast knee of a bronze statue. But the German word for casting, *gießen*, "to pour," recalls the fluidity and liquidity in the frozen cast. The transformation of the sexuality of the flesh into the eroticism of the beautiful statue not only passes through the borderline and twilight zone of the visible and invisible but also hovers between the dismembered body of erogenous zones and the imaginary totality of the beautiful, whole Gestalt, for which Greek sculpture provided, not least through its torsi, the archetypal, specular images.

If the poetic "I" of Baudelaire's poem functions like a Medusa head, or the eye of the Basilisque, the body of this "I/eye" seems to become the victim of its own glance. It is seized by a convulsive cramp: "crispé comme un extravagant." Physiologically, *crisper* is a contraction of muscles and skin. Like Niobe in Hölderlin's translation, "contracted into slow rock," the body of the poetic "I" is seized by a contracting convulsion in the moment of a passing. In this convulsive contraction the poetic "I" presents itself as the poetic body in contrast to the noble restraint of the sculptured body in the sense in which Lessing's Laokoon essay contrasts poetry with sculpture and painting. The latter, frozen in space, should hover in the "pregnant moment," which contracts and condenses the preceding and the following moment, after the attack and before the scream. Poetry, passing through time, can unfold that moment into the sequences of word after word. In poetry, the pregnant moment is ready for the birth pangs of a birth, which, in Baudelaire's poem, literally is a renaissance of the poetic "I" in the glance of a passing vision: "dont le regard m'a fait renaître." But these birth pangs are close to and perhaps indistinguishable from death pangs.

Like Niobe, having become like a desert, the poetic "I/eye" has become a thirsty mouth, drinking from another eye that is at the same time sky and heaven, threatening, promising a storm. It is a moment of multiple transports and transfers: from eye to eye, from eye to mouth, from eye to sky, preparing the pronominal transfer from "I" to "you." The "you" enters in the French text with a deadly homonym as a "plaisir qui tue." The consumption of the erotic moment is the moment of birth and death: the renaissance of the drinking *moi,je* as an apostrophized *m'*, in which the "I" is killed through the *tu(e)*, opening up to the figure of apostrophe through which the poetic 'I" can now address the other: "O toi

..., ô toi." This *ô toi* breaks open the circle of deafening noise around the "I" and its towering erection ("autour de moi") to the silence of a belated knowledge: "ô toi qui le savais."

The transition from the initial noise to the crystalline silence of this knowledge is a Parisian dream: "Tout pour l'oeil, rien pour les oreilles!/Un silence d'éternité." It is the eternity in which alone there is a hope for seeing: "Ne te verrai-je plus que dans l'éternité?"—but only as the belated knowledge that has passed through the possibility of an underlined/italicized *jamais*. In "Le cygne," the thirsting swan cries to the sky for water: "Eau, quand donc pleuvras-tu? quand tonneras-tu, foudre?" In *A une passante,* the lightning has hit and transformed the *eau* of the water into the pure *ô* of address.

Baudelaire's poem inverts the movement of the Greek chorus in *Antigone:* from the narrative of an apparition to the apostrophe of an invisible absence. The Sophoclean chorus begins with the apostrophe and is carried away by the narrative of a stunning apparition. But the two movements lead to the same point of a melancholic knowledge: "ô toi que j'eusse aimée, ô toi qui le savais"— "gêra to phronein edidaxan" [they (the big words in Greek, the great glances in Hölderlin's translation) have taught me to think in old age]. Baudelaire's knowledge is even more devious: the knowledge that a moment, forever passed, carried a knowledge with it.

6

We return, at the end, to the mysterious word *werden* in Benjamin's translation, echoing the equally mysterious *werden* of Hölderlin's Sophocles translation. Both *werden* emerge in the moment of a passing apparition that is also the apparition and passing of beauty. Both are located in the transition from day to night, from life to death. Hölderlin's *werden* invokes the becoming of great understandings in the beginning at a moment when all understanding is suspended. Benjamin's *werdende* seems to claim the becoming of someone who is decomposing ("ich verfiel") through the same eye whose shimmer seems to regenerate him into becoming: "dem Werdenden an ihrem Schimmer."

In contrast to Hölderlin's *werden,* Benjamin's *werden* has a certain semantic correspondence in the French *renaître.* As the French *renaître* emerges from the germination of a potentially deadly storm ("où germe l'ouragan"), the German *werden* emerges from the crumbling and decomposition of the "I" that has fallen over to the eye of the captivating, deadly apparition.

Yet the word *werdenden* might have been generated by a much more literal correspondence of letters between the French *naître* and the German *werden,* invoking in its literality not only the entering into being through *naître* but also its negation: *n'être,* and in the German *werden* the *Erde* that covers the dead through *beerdigen.* Such a literality of the letters is indeed one of the consistent patterns in Benjamin's translations besides his attempt at rendering the French syntax and Baudelaire's rhyme schemes as precisely as possible. To be sure, this literality of the letters is restrained. Despite the radical claim for the displacement of meaning by the literality of syntax that privileges the word in the preface on the task of the translator, Benjamin's praxis of translation remains within a controlled compromise formation both in the literality of syntax and of letters. But the latter is strongly employed wherever feasible: "germe l'ouragan : vorm Orkan."

With "dem Werdenden an ihrem Schimmer," the compromise formation of the translation is pushed toward the limit of semantic understanding. But at this limit the kernel of the preface on the task of the translator is silhouetted in a knot of overdeterminations: the word *werden* points at the *werden* of the "Werden der Sprache selbst" through the pure word.

En archê ên ho logos: Benjamin quotes these words of the beginning of the Gospel according to John in Greek and translates them into German: "im Anfang war das Wort" (4:18). He quotes it as a law also for translation. At the end of a powerful reading of Benjamin's essay, Carol Jacobs suggests that Benjamin's text might be read as a translation of these lines from the Holy Writ.[16] It seems that this translation is continued in the translations of Baudelaire, whose decomposed name passes, fleetingly, through the *éclair* of *beauté.*

The logos of John's Gospel goes through a sequence of qualifications and translations. Like the *himeros* of the Sophoclean chorus, he is placed at the beginning with the highest principle, with the institution of the laws in Sophocles (which, in Hölderlin's translation, are the principle of the generation of understanding), with God (*pros theon*) in the text of John. This being of the logos with God seems first of all to displace God from himself, when the text continues *kai theos ên ho logos,* God was the logos. From the beginning, then, God did not become logos, but was it already. It is now this being of logos that is declared the principle of all genesis, of all becoming: *werden.* "Panta di' autou egeneto, kai chôris autou egeneto oude hen, ho gegonen" [Everything became through him (the logos), and outside of him not one thing that became became]. The logos thus is the principle of *werden.* And he is also the place of life (*en autô zôê ên*), which in turn is called light (*kai zôê ên to phôs*). It is said of this light that it shines in the darkness, and darkness either did not take a hold of it, did not overpower it, or did not comprehend it (the word *katelaben* is ambivalent, meaning seizing something, both in the sense of taking something over, overcoming, and comprehending). Such multivalence is, of course, the very effect of the word as the generating principle of significations and their transports through translations and metaphors.

Hölderlin's translation, as we have seen, transferred Eros and *himeros*, respectively, to the place of the creative breath of the Elohim hovering over the waters, and to the beginning where the logos according to John was with God and according to Hölderlin as powerfully begging desire participating in the generation of understanding. This presence of the logos in the desire, appearing through the batting of the eyelid that produces the glance, is underlined in Hölderlin's translation of *logoi* as *Blike.*

The glance of the eye shifts in the German cognate *Glanz* into the shining of a light which leaves in Benjamin's translation a shimmering that seems to effect the becoming: "dem Werdenden an ihrem Schimmer." This becoming is preceded by a fall, a falling over to the eye, a falling to pieces of the poetic "I": "Und ich verfiel in Krampf und Siechtum an/Dies Aug' den fahlen Himmel vorm Orkan/Und habe Lust zum Tode dran genossen." The syntax moves along, without a single punctuation mark. Without the pause of a comma the eye glides into the sky, and the "I" into the deadly *jouissance*. Benjamin's translation seems to be seized at this moment by the innermost momentum of a translation where the sense, as in Hölderlin's Sophocles translations, "plunges from abyss to abyss until it threatens to be lost in bottomless depths of language."

Benjamin claims a stop and a hold: *ein Halten,* provided only by the Holy Writ, which offers, however, no meaning because "meaning has stopped to be the water shed between flowing language and flowing revelation." It is the radical liquification of all meaning in the waters over which the Elohim, Eros, and logos hover, with the polyonymous creator of names Dionysus, from translation to translation.

The light shines in the darkness. Meanings emerge. Love stories take place. But the light cannot be apprehended or comprehended; it does not lend itself to anything that becomes under its lightning bolt; meaning glides over in other meanings; accents are shifted; love stories come to an end, or perhaps are simply translated into other stories, other texts. Between them, intertextually, through translations, the kernel of pure language attempts "to present, even to produce itself."

Notes

INTRODUCTION

Epigraphs: Baudelaire, *Les paradis artificiels,* in *Oeuvres complètes,* Bibliothèque de la Pléiade (Paris: Gallimard, 1975), 1:506. Barthes, *Le plaisir du texte* (Paris: Editions du Seuil, 1973), 10. Nietzsche, *Sämtliche Werke: Kritische Studienausgabe,* ed. Giorgio Colli and Mazzino Montinari (Munich: Deutscher Taschenbuchverlag, 1980), 1:888.

1. The entry is August 2, 1914, in Franz Kafka, *Tagebücher: Kritische Ausgabe* (Frankfurt am Main: S. Fischer, 1990), 543.

2. Friedrich Hölderlin, *Essays and Letters on Theory,* translated and edited by Thomas Pfau (Albany: State University of New York Press, 1988), 111.

3. How much of Derrida's philosophy is shaped by a deconstructive reading of a philosophical tradition of reflection has been shown by Rodolphe Gasché, *The Tain of the Mirror: Derrida and the Philosophy of Reflection* (Cambridge: Harvard University Press, 1986).

4. Jürgen Habermas, "Selbstreflexion als Wissenschaft: Freuds psychoanalytische Sinnkritik," in *Erkenntnis und Interesse* (Frankfurt am Main: Suhrkamp, 1973), 262–300.

5. Jürgen Habermas, *Der philosophische Diskurs der Moderne* (Frankfurt am Main: Suhrkamp, 1985). English translation: *The Philosophical Discourse of Modernity* (Cambridge: MIT Press, 1987).

6. "Meine Selbstanalyse bleibt unterbrochen. Ich habe eingesehen, warum. Ich kann mich nur selbst analysieren mit den objektiv gewonnenen Kenntnissen (wie ein Fremder), eigentliche Selbstanalyse ist unmöglich." Letter to Wilhelm Fließ, November 14, 1897. Sigmund Freud, *Briefe an Wilhelm Fließ, 1887–1904* (Frankfurt am Main: S. Fischer, 1986), 305.

7. "Erstens gibt es keine seelische Verhaltensweise im Sinne irgend einer von Grund aus von leiblicher wesensverschiednen. . . . Die angebliche Differenz, daß fremdes Seelenleben uns im Gegensatz zum eignen nur mittelbar durch Deutung fremder Leiblichkeit gegeben sei besteht nicht. . . . Fremdes Seelenleben wird nicht prinzipiell anders als eignes wahrgenommen, es wird nicht erschlossen, sondern im Leiblichen, das ihm als Seelenleben zugehört, gesehen." (Walter Benjamin, *Gesammelte Schriften,* Hrsg. v. Rolf Tiedemann u. Hermann Schweppenhäuser (Frankfurt am Main: Suhrkamp, 1980), 6:65. All quotations of Benjamin are from this edition.

8. Translation by Beryl Schlossman.

9. Typical correspondences between the macrocosmos and microcosmos in the pansophic world of the sixteenth and seventeenth centuries would relate, for example, sun-gold-heart; moon-silver-brain; Jupiter-tin-liver.

10. What I call here the "fetishization" of theory is by no means limited to so-called theoretical critics; on the contrary, it exerts its power often most strongly over those who consider themselves atheoretical or antitheoretical. This can be anecdotally illustrated in the job search of a large literature department where the large majority considers itself 'traditional' (a slightly euphemistic term for conventional), with the exception of one member who was hired, in the name of pluralism, as a representative of 'theory'. When a few years later another position opens up, a highly original candidate with several stunning publications is eliminated at the beginning with the argument: "We already have a theoretician," although the work and interests of this candidate are radically different from the other 'theoretician' in the department. The argument strongly reminds one of the worn-out joke of the man who refuses a highly recommended book with the argument: "But I already have a book at home."

11. Judith Still and Michael Worton, introduction to *Intertextuality: Theories and Practices* (Manchester: Manchester University Press, 1990), 17.

12. The most concise discussion of the necessary generalization of the concept of 'text' can be found in Jacques Derrida, *Positions* (Chicago: University of Chicago Press, 1971). See also Gasché's excellent exegesis of the concept in *Tain of the Mirror*, 278–93.

13. Jacques Derrida, *Of Grammatology* (Baltimore: Johns Hopkins University Press, 1976), 158.

14. "Das Dasein der Sprache erstreckt sich aber nicht nur über alle Gebiete menschlicher Geistesäußerung, der in irgendeinem Sinne immer Sprache innewohnt, sondern es erstreckt sich auf schlechthin alles." Walter Benjamin, "Über die Sprache überhaupt und über die Sprache des Menschen," 2:140.

15. Gasché, *Tain of the Mirror*, 279.

16. "Die Ansicht, daß das geistige Wesen eines Dinges eben in seiner Sprache besteht—diese Ansicht als Hypothesis verstanden, ist der große Abgrund, dem alle Sprachtheorie zu verfallen droht, und über, gerade über ihm sich schwebend zu erhalten ist ihre Aufgabe" (2:141).

17. "Classical" and "modern" are used here more in a typological than a historical sense.

18. Peter Szondi, *Theorie des modernen Dramas,* in *Schriften I* (Frankfurt am Main: Suhrkamp, 1970), 10–148.

19. Benjamin, 2:519.

20. Ibid.

21. "L'Autre, l'Inconscient, est ici dans ce creux, ce vide autour duquel tournent en rond plusieurs langues." Daniel Sibony, *La juive: Une transmission d'inconscient* (Paris: Editions Grasset & Fasquelle, 1983), 59. See also Elisabeth Weber, "Eigensinn," in *Wahnwelten im Zusammenstoß: Die Psychose als Spiegel der Zeit,* ed. D. Kamper and U. Sonneman (Berlin: Akademie Verlag, 1993), 109.

22. "Wie nämlich Scherben eines Gefäßes, um sich zusammenfügen zu lassen, in den kleinsten Einzelheiten einander zu folgen, doch nicht so zu gleichen haben, so muß anstatt dem Sinn des Originals sich ähnlich zu machen, die Übersetzung liebend vielmehr und bis ins Einzelne hinein dessen Art des Meinens in der eigenen Sprache sich anbilden, um so beide wie Scherben als Bruchstück eines Gefäßes, als Bruchstück einer größeren Sprache erkennbar zu machen" (4:18). My translation follows here, with slight modification, Carol Jacobs' translation in "The Monstrosity of Translation: Walter Benjamin's 'The Task of the Translator,'" in *Telling Time: Lévi-Strauss, Ford, Lessing, Benjamin, de Man, Wordsworth, Rilke* (Baltimore: Johns Hopkins University Press, 1992), 136.

23. On Heine's and Baudelaire's relationship to modernity, see Theodor W. Adorno, "Die Wunde Heine," in idem, *Gesammelte Schriften,* ed. Rolf Tiedemann (Frankfurt am Main: Suhrkamp, 1974), vol. 11: *Noten zur Literatur,* 95–100.

24. "Die 'Harzreise' ist und bleibt Fragment, und die bunten Fäden, die so hübsch hineingesponnen sind, um sich im Ganzen harmonisch zu verschlingen, werden plötzlich, wie von der Schere der Parze, abgeschnitten. Vielleicht verwebe ich sie weiter in künftigen Liedern, und was jetzt kärglich verschwiegen ist, wird alsdann vollauf gesagt. Am Ende kommt es auch auf eins heraus, wann und wo man etwas ausgesprochen hat, wenn man es nur überhaupt einmal ausspricht. Mögen die einzelnen Werke immerhin Fragmente bleiben, wenn sie nur in ihrer Vereinigung ein Ganzes bilden." Heinrich Heine, "Die Harzreise," in idem, *Sämtliche Schriften,* ed. Klaus Briegleb (Munich: Hanser, 1969), 2:162.

25. Barthes, *Le plaisir de texte,* 11 ff.

26. "Über Wahrheit und Lüge im aussermoralischen Sinne," in *Sämtliche Werke,* 1:873–90.

27. French critics played a major role in the rereading of this essay. The issue of *Poétique* 5 (1971), with essays by Derrida ("La mythologie

blanche"), Philippe Lacoue-Labarthe ("Le détour"), and Sarah Kofman ("Nietzsche et la métaphore"), was as seminal as the following Nietzsche colloquium of Cérisy-la-Salle in 1972.

28. "Was ist also Wahrheit? Ein bewegliches Heer von Metaphern, Metonymien, Anthropomorphismen, kurz eine Summe von menschlichen Relationen, die, poetisch und rhetorisch gesteigert, übertragen, geschmückt wurden, und die nach langem Gebrauche einem Volke fest, canonisch und verbindlich dünken: die Wahrheiten sind Illusionen, von denen man vergessen hat, dass sie welche sind, Metaphern, die abgenutzt und sinnlich kraftlos geworden sind, Münzen, die ihr Bild verloren haben und nun als Metall, nicht mehr als Münzen in Betracht kommen." Nietzsche, "Über Wahrheit," 1:880 ff. (my translation in the text).

29. Habermas, *Der philosophische Diskurs der Moderne.*

30. Not even the pages of the *New York Review of Books* recoil in shame when Geoffrey Hartman is condescendingly patted on the shoulder and assured that his longtime occupation with the Holocaust saves him, despite some taintedness with deconstruction, from the idolatry of language and words. Perhaps it has never occurred to these literary rhetoricians and their moral pathos that the Holocaust was an attempt at an annihilation of a people and culture where the letter stood and stands in highest regard, and that it was not least this reverence for the letter that fed the rhetoric of Christian anti-Semitism since Saint Paul and Saint Augustine.

31. "Das Lebendige in der Poesie ist jezt dasjenige, was am meisten meine Gedanken und Sinne beschäfftiget. Ich fühle so tief, wie weit ich noch davon bin, es zu treffen." Friedrich Hölderlin, *Sämtliche Werke,* Große Stuttgarter Ausgabe (Stuttgart: Kohlhammer, 1943–1974 6:289. Hereafter this edition is cited as StA.

32. In his second letter to Böhlendorff, Hölderlin refers to himself as one who has been hit and struck by Apollo: "daß mich Apollo geschlagen" (StA 6:432).

33. Also in the first chorus part of *Oedipus* (v. 167): *phoibon hekabolon,* which Hölderlin translates as "den Phöbus fernhin treffend." Friedrich Hölderlin, *Sämtliche Werke,* Frankfurter Ausgabe (Frankfurt am Main: Roter Stern, 1979), 16:97. Hereafter this edition is cited as FA.

34. For the Pindaric connotations and their traces in Hölderlin's poetry, see Albert Seifert, *Untersuchungen zu Hölderlins Pindar-Rezeption* (Munich: Fink, 1982), 210 ff.

35. "Nicht so ist es, daß das Vergangene sein Licht auf das Gegenwärtige oder das Gegenwärtige sein Licht auf das Vergangene wirft, son-

dern Bild ist dasjenige, worin das Gewesene mit dem Jetzt blitzhaft zu einer Konstellation zusammentritt. Mit andern Worten: Bild ist die Dialektik im Stillstand" (5:576 ff.; N 2a, 3).

36. "Wenn der Dichter einmal des Geistes mächtig," FA 14:319.

37. Bertolt Brecht, *Gesammelte Werke* (Frankfurt am Mann: Suhrkamp, 1967), 19:398.

38. Ibid., 15:245.

39. Ibid., 16:612.

40. Benjamin's essay "Der Sürrealismus" was published in 1929, now in *Gesammelte Schriften*, 2:295–310.

41. Ibid., 2:297.

42. See the excellent reading of this text by Claire Lyu, *Transpoetry: Voices, Conjunctions, and Spaces in Baudelaire* (Ph.D. diss., Johns Hopkins University, 1994).

43. 2:296 ff.

44. "Sie liegt in einer *profanen Erleuchtung,* einer materialistischen, anthropologischen Inspiration, zu der Haschisch, Opium und was immer sonst die Vorschule abgeben können. (Aber eine gefährliche. Und die der Religion ist strenger.)" Ibid., 2:297.

45. "Als solche gehört die Idee einem grundsätzlich andern Bereich an als das von ihr Erfaßte" (1:214).

46. "Die Ideen verhalten sich zu den Dingen wie die Sternbilder zu den Sternen. Das besagt zunächst: sie sind weder deren Begriffe noch deren Gesetze" (1:214).

47. 1:208.

48. 1:125.

49. See, for example, Benjamin's letter to Gretel Adorno: "Das dialektische Bild malt den Traum nicht nach—das zu behaupten lag niemals in meiner Absicht. Wohl aber scheint es mir, die Instanzen, die Einbruchsstelle des Erwachens zu enthalten, ja aus diesen Stellen seine Figur wie ein Sternbild aus den leuchtenden Punkten erst herzustellen" [The dialectical image does not depict the dream—it was never my intention to claim that. But it seems to me to contain the agencies, the rupturing points of awakening and to construct from these points its figure like a star constellation is made out of its luminous points]. Benjamin to Gretel Adorno, August 16, 1935, in Adorno and Benjamin, *Briefwechsel, 1928–1940* (Frankfurt am Main: Suhrkamp, 1994), 157.

50. "Nur dialektische Bilder sind echte (d.h. nicht archaische) Bilder; und der Ort, an dem man sie antrifft, ist die Sprache" [Only dialectical images are genuine (i.e., not archaic) images; and the place where one encounters them is language]. Benjamin, *Gesammelte Schriften*, 5:577.

51. Kafka, *Tagebücher*, 594.

52. Ibid., 596.

53. Sigmund Freud, "Konstruktionen in der Analyse" (1937), in *Studienausgabe: Ergänzungsband: Schriften zur Behandlungstechnik* (Frankfurt am Main: S. Fischer, 1975), 393–406.

CHAPTER I: ECHOLALIA

Epigraph: Blanchot, "La littérature et le droit à la mort," in *De Kafka à Kafka* (Paris: Gallimard, 1981), 46.

1. "*Sie* [die Aufgabe des Übersetzers] besteht darin, diejenige Intention auf die Sprache, in die übersetzt wird, zu finden, von der aus in ihr das Echo des Originals erweckt wird. . . . Die Übersetzung aber sieht sich nicht wie die Dichtung gleichsam im innern Bergwald der Sprache selbst, sondern außerhalb desselben, ihm gegenüber und ohne ihn zu betreten ruft sie das Original hinein, an demjenigen einzigen Ort hinein, wo jeweils das Echo in der eigenen den Widerhall eines Werkes der fremden Sprache zu geben vermag." Walter Benjamin, *Gesammelte Schriften,* ed. Rolf Tiedemann and Hermann Schweppenhäuser (Frankfurt am Main: Suhrkamp, 1980), 4:16. All Benjamin quotations are from this edition. Translations, if not otherwise indicated, are my own.

2. Walter Benjamin, *Illuminations,* trans. Harry Zohn (New York: Schocken Books, 1969), 76.

3. Carol Jacobs, "The Monstrosity of Translation: Walter Benjamin's 'The Task of the Translator,'" in *Telling Time: Lévi-Strauss, Ford, Lessing, Benjamin, de Man, Wordsworth, Rilke* (Baltimore: Johns Hopkins University Press, 1993), 128–41.

4. Paul de Man, "Walter Benjamin's 'The Task of the Translator,'" in *The Resistance to Theory* (Minneapolis: University of Minnesota Press, 1987), 73–105.

5. Ibid., 103.

6. Ibid., 86.

7. "Treue in der Übersetzung des einzelnen Wortes kann fast nie den Sinn voll wiedergeben, den es im Original hat. Denn dieser erschöpft sich nach seiner dichterischen Bedeutung fürs Original nicht in dem Gemeinten, sondern gewinnt diese gerade dadurch, wie das Gemeinte an die Art des Meinens in dem bestimmten Worte gebunden ist. Man pflegt dies in der Formel auszudrücken, daß die Worte einen Gefühlston mit sich führen" (4:17).

8. For the resonances of this 'tone', see also Menninghaus: "The expression of the 'tone' of a language is as widespread as it is difficult to explicate. One understands with the 'tone' of a language something that

is not determined by the 'verbal contents,' but something that is effected 'immediately' 'in' them. Especially well known is the ironic tone that expresses something that is not only not contained in any of the contents, but is even opposed to them." Winfried Menninghaus, *Walter Benjamins Theorie der Sprachmagie* (Frankfurt am Main: Suhrkamp, 1980), 13.

9. On the tradition and significance of echoes in literature and rhetoric see John Hollander, *The Figure of Echo: A Mode of Allusion in Milton and After* (Berkeley: University of California Press, 1981).

10. Most extensively by Menninghaus, *Walter Benjamins Theorie der Sprachmagie.*

11. What irrupts in Hölderlin as the violent and powerful fate of the word into the occidental world has become dust and ashes in Baudelaire's poetry, but out of the ashes still resonates the vocation of the poet: "Mon berceau s'adossait à la bibliothèque,/Babel sombre, où roman, science, fabliau,/Tout, la cendre latine et la poussière grecque,/Se mêlaient" [My cradle stood near the bookshelves, a sombre Babel, where everything: novels, science, fables, the Latin ashes and the Greek dust mingled] ("La voix," vv. 1–4).

12. It is curious that Benjamin names Hölderlin's Sophocles translations and not his translations of Pindar as paradigms for interlinear translation; in the strict sense, only the latter are interlinear. It seems, then, that for Benjamin interlinearity is only a heuristic approximation to the ideal of a complementary harmony between languages, which Benjamin finds in Hölderlin's Sophocles translations: "In ihnen ist die Harmonie der Sprachen so tief, daß der Sinn nur noch wie eine Äolsharfe vom Winde von der Sprache berührt wird" [In them the harmony of the languages is so profound that meaning in them is touched only lightly like an Aeolian harp by the wind] (4:21). This harmony cannot appear on the phenomenal level.

13. "In ihnen stürzt der Sinn von Abgrund zu Abgrund, bis er droht in bodenlosen Sprachtiefen sich zu verlieren" (4:21).

14. "Die kontemplative Ruhe, mit welcher sie [Allegorie] in den Abgrund zwischen bildlichem Sein und Bedeuten sich versenkt" (1:342).

15. "Schrift und Laut stehen in hochgespannter Polarität einander gegenüber. . . . Die Kluft zwischen bedeutendem Schriftbild und berauschendem Sprachlaut nötigt, wie deas gefestete Massiv der Worbedeutung in ihr aufgerissen wird, den Blick in die Sprachtiefe" (1:376).

16. "Die Ansicht, daß das geistige Wesen eines Dinges eben in seiner Sprache besteht—diese Ansicht als Hypothesis verstanden, ist der große

Abgrund, dem alle Sprachtheorie zu verfallen droht, und über, gerade über ihm sich schwebend zu erhalten ist ihre Aufgabe" (2:141).

17. Beißner, the editor of the Stuttgart edition, calculated the measure of the empty space on the page as approximately twenty-four verses and lets the poem 'begin' with line 25.

18. See, for example, the tables in FA 14:336–37.

19. This makes it so difficult, if not impossible, to determine the "tone" of a specific passage of poem on the basis of semantic determinants.

20. "Die Fühlbarkeit des Ganzen schreitet also in eben dem Grade und Verhältnisse fort, in welchem die Trennung in den Theilen und ihrem Centrum, worin die Theile und das Ganze am fühlbarsten sind, fortschreitet." FA 14:371.

21. "Wiederklang der ursprünglichen lebendigen Empfindung . . . in diesem Augenblicke ist es, wo man sagen kann, daß die Sprache geahndet wird." FA 14:319. The German word for resonance or echo is usually written Widerklang, literally: "countersound"; but Hölderlin writes Wiederklang and thus accentuates the repetition of the sound as a resounding.

22. "So wie die Erkenntniß die Sprache ahndet, so erinnert sich die Sprache der Erkenntniß." FA 14:319.

23. "Und eben diese [die reine, die wahre Sprache], in deren Ahnung und Beschreibung die einzige Vollkommenheit liegt, welche der Philosoph erhoffen kann, sie ist intensive in den Übersetzungen verborgen" (4:16).

24. "Der als Eigenstes es zufällt, auf jene Nachreife des fremden Wortes, auf die Wehen des eigenen zu merken" (4:13).

25. De Man, "Walter Benjamin's 'The Task of the Translator,'" 85.

26. Ibid., 84.

27. Bertolt Brecht, "Vom ertrunkenen Mächen," in Große kommentierte Berliner und Frankfurter Ausgabe, vol. 11, Gedichte I (Berlin: Suhrkamp Verlag, 1988), 109.

28. "In den Anagrammen, den onomatopoetischen Wendungen und vielen Sprachkunststücken anderer Art stolziert das Wort, die Silbe und der Laut emanzipiert von jeder hergebrachten Sinnverbindung, als Ding, das allegorisch ausgebeutet werden darf. . . . Dergestalt wird die Sprache zerbrochen, um in ihren Bruchstücken sich einem veränderten und gesteigerten Ausdruck zu leihen. . . . Die zertrümmerte Sprache hat in ihren Stücken aufgehört, bloßer Mitteilung zu dienen und stellt als neugeborner Gegenstand seine Würde neben die der Götter, Flüsse, Tugenden und ähnlicher, ins Allegorische hinüberschillernder Naturgestalten" (1:381 ff.).

29. "Wie nämlich Scherben eines Gefäßes, um sich zusammenfügen zu lassen, in den kleinsten Einzelheiten einander zu folgen, doch nicht so zu gleichen haben, so muß anstatt dem Sinn des Originals sich ähnlich zu machen, die Übersetzung liebend vielmehr und bis ins Einzelne hinein dessen Art des Meinens in der eigenen Sprache sich anbilden, um so beide wie Scherben als Bruchstück eines Gefäßes, als Bruchstück einer größeren Sprache erkennbar zu machen" (4:18). My translation follows here, with slight modification, Carol Jacobs' translation in *Telling Time*, 136.

30. "Wenn nun gerade das Echo, die eigentliche Domäne eines freien Lautspiels, von Bedeutung sozusagen befallen wird, so mußte vollends dies als eine Offenbarung des Sprachlichen, wie jene Zeit es fühlte, sich erweisen" (1:384).

31. "Das stilistische Gesetz des Schwulstes, die Formel von 'Asiatischen Worten'" (1:384). The expression "Asiatische Worte" is a quotation from the baroque writer Hallmann, which in turn takes up the ancient opposition of a restrained classical style versus the excess and bombast of Asian style (*stylus Asiaticus*).

32. *Wörtlichkeit in der Übertragung der Syntax* (4:18).

33. "Wo der Sinn aufgehört hat, die Wasserscheide für die strömende Sprache und die strömende Offenbarung zu sein," (4:21).

34. "Die Treue ist der Rhythmus der emanatistisch absteigenden Intentionsstufen, in welcher die aufsteigenden der neuplatonischen Theosophie beziehugnsvoll verwandelt sich abspiegeln" (1:334).

35. Maurice Blanchot, "La voix narrative," in *De Kafka à Kafka*, 184.

36. "Den Sinn in sein verborgenes und, wenn man so sagen darf, waldiges Innere aufnimmt" (1:342).

37. See Hans-Jörg Spitz, *Die Metaphorik des geistigen Schriftsinns: Ein Beitrag zur allegorischen Bibelauslegung des ersten christlichen Jahrtausends* (Munich: Fink, 1972), 132: "die *vastitas* und *universitas* der *sacra historia* vergleicht Gregor riesigen, an Berge grenzenden Wäldern, die sich zwar von hoher Warte überschauen lassen, über deren wirkliche Weite der Betrachter jedoch getäuscht wird, zumal ihm die Schluchten und Ebenen in der verkürzten Perspecktive verborgen bleiben müssen."

38. Hieronymus Lauretus (Jerónimo Lloret), *Silva Allegoriarum Totius Sacrae Scripturae* (Barcelona, 1570; Cologne, 1681, photomechanical reprint: Munich: Fink, 1971).

39. See also the commentary of Friedrich Ohly in the introduction to the reprint of the *Silva* (see n. 38), 9.

40. "Eine Metapher aber ist das Wort 'Sprache' in solchem Gebrauche durchaus nicht. Denn es ist eine volle inhaltliche Erkenntnis, daß wir uns nichts vorstellen können, das sein geistiges Wesen nicht im Ausdruck mitteilt" (2:141).

41. "In völlig unmetaphorischer Sachlichkeit" (4:11).

42. "Während der Lehrgehalt von Kafkas Stücken in der Form der Parabel zum Vorschein kommt, bekundet ihr symbolischer Gehalt sich im Gestus. Die eigentliche Antinomie von Kafkas Werk liegt im Verhältnis von Gleichnis und Symbol" (2:1255).

43. "So war für Kafka sicher am unabsehbarsten der Gestus" (2:419).

44. Jacobs, *Telling Time*, 137.

45. Jacques Derrida, "Des tours de Babel," in *Psyché: Invention de l'autre* (Paris: Galilée, 1987), 222.

46. "Einen Tisch mit peinlich ordentlicher Handwerksmäßigkeit zusammenzuhämmern und dabei gleichzeitig nichts zu tun undzwar nicht so daß man sagen könnte: 'ihm ist das Hämmern ein Nichts, sondern 'ihm ist das Hämmern ein wirkliches Hämmern und gleichzeitig auch ein Nichts', wodurch ja das Hämmern noch kühner, noch entschlossener, noch wirklicher und wenn Du willst noch irrsinniger geworden wäre." Franz Kafka, *Tagebücher: Kritische Ausgabe* (Frankfurt am Main: S. Fischer, 1990), 855.

47. Baudelaire, *Oeuvres Complètes*, Bibliothèque de la Pléiade (Paris: Gallimard, 1975), 1:399.

48. On the meaning of the name Babel, see Derrida, "Des tours de Babel," 204. Luther, in his translation of the Bible, also points out this meaning: "Auf Deudsch Ein vermischung oder verwirrung" [In German a mixing together or confusion].

49. "So bleibt ihm [dem Sinn] ganz nah und doch unendlich fern, unter ihm verborgen oder deutlicher, durch ihn gebrochen oder machtvoller über alle Mitteilung hinaus ein Letztes, Entscheidendes. Es bleibt in aller Sprache und ihren Gebilden außer dem Mitteilbaren ein Nicht-Mitteilbares, ein, je nach dem Zusammenhang, in dem es angetroffen wird, Symbolisierendes oder Symbolisiertes" (4:18 ff.).

CHAPTER 2: RECALLING THE GODS
Die scheinheiligen Dichter
1. Ihr kalten Heuchler, sprecht von den Göttern nicht!
Ihr habt Verstand! ihr glaubt nicht an Helios,
Noch an den Donnerer und Meergott;
Todt ist die Erde, wer mag ihr danken?—

Getrost ihr Götter! zieret ihr doch das Lied,
   Wenn schon aus euren Nahmen die Seele schwand,
      Und ist ein großes Wort vonnöthen,
         Mutter Natur! so gedenkt man deiner. FA 5:538.

2. Reduced to the cliché, Detlev Lüders' commentary on Hölderlin's poems is symptomatic: "Das Gedicht ["Die Scheinheiligen Dichter"] wendet sich gegen den nur allegorischen Gebrauch der Götternamen, der in so vielen Dichtungen des 18. Jahrhunderts herrscht und seinen Grund in dem Verlust des Glaubens an die Realität der Götter hat." Friedrich Hölderlin, *Sämtliche Gedichte: Studienausgabe in zwei Bänden*, Hrsg. u. kommentiert von Detlev Lüders (Homburg: Athenäum Verlag, 1970), 2:145.

3. Hölderlin was sensitive to such interlinguistic echoes and occasionally lets them resound in his poetry, such as the echo of the Greek *Aithêr* and the German *heiter* in "Brod und Wein": "Vater Aether! so riefs . . . Vater! heiter! und hallt" (vv. 65–69).

4. With a more spatial emphasis, Jean Bollack translates the line as "j'en atteste le dieu posté devant tous les dieux, Soleil." Jean Bollack, *L'Oedipe Roi de Sophocle* (Lille: Presses Universitaires de Lille, 1990), 1:229.

5. The link between *vorstellen* and *danken* is articulated most explicitly in a text that Beißner edited under the title "Über Religion" and which Sattler brings in close connection with the so-called *Systemprogramm* of German idealism as "Fragment of Philosophical Letters." The fragment opens with the question "warum sie [die Menschen] sich den Zusammenhang zwischen sich und ihrer Welt gerade *vorstellen*, warum sie sich eine Idee oder ein Bild machen müssen" [why human beings have to *represent* to themselves the relation between themselves and the world, why they have to produce an idea or image of it] and answers: "daß der Mensch auch in so fern sich über die Noth erhebt, als er sich seines Geschiks *erinnern*, als er für sein Leben *dankbar* seyn kann" [that man rises above necessity insofar as he can *remember* his fate, as he can be *thankful* for his life]. FA 14:46.

6. E. R. Curtius, *European Literature and the Latin Middle Ages* (Princeton: Princeton University Press, 1973), 106 ff.

7. Half a century earlier Klopstock celebrated the beauty of "Mother Nature's" inventions in his poem "Der Zürichsee" [1750] ("Schön ist, Mutter Natur, deiner Erfindungen Pracht"), but her beauty is confronted with the higher beauty of the "great thought, thinking again [her] creations." Poetic thought and feeling become a second creation investing the allegorical figure of Mother Nature with another legitima-

tion that will lead in the new poetics to a denunciation of allegory in the name of 'genuine' poetic feeling: *Empfindung*.

8. Walter Benjamin, *Gesammelte Schriften*, Hrsg. v. Rolf Tiedemann u. Hermann Schweppenhäuser (Frankfurt am Main: Suhrkamp, 1980), 6:15. All quotations of Benjamin are cited from this edition.

9. See, for example, Theodor Vischer's critique of Goethe's *Faust II*: F. Theodor Vischer, "Die Litterature über Göthe's Faust: Eine Übersicht," in *Goethe im Urteil seiner Kritiker: Dokumente zur Wirkungsgeschichte Goethes in Deutschland*, p. 2, 1832–70, ed. Karl Robert Mandelkow (Munich: C. H. Beck, 1977), 184 ff.

10. Benjmain, 1:394.

11. This precariousness is not lessened, rather increased, by Heidegger's commentary of the poem and its historical insensitivity.

12. In his transcription of the manuscript in the *Homburger Folioheft*, D. E. Sattler marks the word *damals* as crossed out. However, the photograph of the manuscript does not show it. Beißner also keeps it in the text, and the poetic logic supports it fully.

13. Hölderlin translates: "bin ich bei Dirzes Wald, Ismenos Gewässer" [I am here with Dirke's forest and Ismenos' waters] FA 17:628–29, 635. The addition of "Wald" signals the other "modern" topography besides the graphematic lines of the rivers and waters that characterize the occidental absence and re-presentation of the gods in Hölderlin's poetry.

14. On this relation with the water, see Bernhard Böschenstein: "Als Wein-Gott ist Dionysos der lösende Gott, der alle trennenden Verfestigungen zwischen den einzelnen Menschen und zwischen den Zeiten aufbricht und in einem Erinnerungsstrom überbrückt. Wenn in der 2. Strophe [des letzten Chorlieds der Antigone], im größten Unterschied zum Original, die 'Wasser' des Cocytus 'bacchantischer fallen,' so gibt es auch heir für Hölderlin eine selbstverständliche Allianz zwischen Dionysos und dem Wasser. Da Hölderlin *nympha* fälschlich mit Wasser, statt mit Nymphe oder Braut wiedergibt, kann man umgekehrt argumentieren und die von ihm übersetzten 'bacchantisch' fallenden Wasser als eine weitere Voraussetzung zu seiner Verbindung des Weingotts mit dem Wasser sehen, statt als eine Folge dieser Vorstellung." Bernhard Böschenstein, *"Frucht des Gewitters": Zu Hölderlins Dionysos als Gott der Revolution* (Frankfurt am Main: Insel, 1989), 22.

15. This is not an unusual phenomenon in the history of linguistic transformations. See, e.g., English: *horse*—German: *Ross;* English: *pot*—German: *Topf;* Greek: *morphê*—Latin: *forma*.

16. Beißner drops the second part of this verse. In the manuscript, Hölderlin underlined "den Abgrund," which could mean that he was not

quite satisfied with the formulation and marked it for a possible future revision. However, there is no indication that he actually dropped it.

17. The parallel was recognized some time ago. Henri Grégoire comments extensively on it and expands the parallels in his edition of the *Bacchae: "spendetai* est passif, comme le reconnaît enfin la dernière édition (la neuvième) de Liddell and Scott. Dodds a parfaitement raison de citer S. Paul, 2 Tim. 4,6 . . . auquel Liddell-Scott ajoute Philip. 2,17. La conversion d'Euripide apparaît d'une manière éclatante dans cette formule eucharistique, sur laquelle Roger Goossens termine son livre posthume, dont les dernières pages furent écrits avant 1939. Cet emploi tout à fait insolite du passif de *spendô* appliqué à une personne à la fois dans les *Bacchantes* et dans deux *Epîtres* n'est pas la seule concordance entre la langue de ce drame et celle du Nouveau Testament: *theomachein,* un verbe 'rather rare', dit Dodds, se lit trois fois dans les *Bacchantes* (45, 325, 1255) et *theomachos* dans les *Actes,* 5,39. Et *pros kentra laktizein* 'se cabrer contre l'aiguillon', se trouve dans les *Bacchantes* 795, et dans les *Actes* 26,14." Euripide, *Tome VI: Bacchai/Les Bacchantes,* texte établi e traduit par Henri Grégoire (Paris: Société d'Édition "Les Belles Lettres," 1973), 253.

18. Cf. Grimm, *Deutsches Wörterbuch.*

19. "houtos de Haidês kai Dionysos" (fragment 15).

20. Benjamin, 1:293 (my translation). For the importance of the death of Socrates for the modern imagination, see also Nietzsche's presentation of it in *The Birth of Tragedy:* "Daß aber der Tod und nicht die Verbannung über ihn ausgesprochen wurde, das scheint Sokrates selbst, mit völliger Klarheit und ohne den natürlichen Schauder vor dem Tode, durchgesetzt zu haben: er ging in den Tod, mit jener Ruhe, mit der er nach Platos Schilderung als der letzte Zecher im frühen Tagesgrauen das Symposion verläßt, um einen neuen Tag zu beginnen; indes hinter ihm, auf den Bänken und auf der Erde, die verschlafenen Tischgenossen zurückbleiben, um von Sokrates, dem wahrhaften Erotiker, zu träumen. *Der sterbende Sokrates* wurde das neue, noch nie sonst geschaute Ideal der edlen griechischen Jugend." Friedrich Nietzsche, *Werke in drei Bänden,* ed. Karl Schlechta (Munich: Carl Hanser, 1966), 1:78.

21. Friedrich Hölderlin, *Homburger Folioheft* (Frankfurt am Main: Stroemfeld/Roterstern, 1986).

22. Commentators have long seen the echo of Bürger's ballad "Lenore" where the ironic identity of bridal bed and coffin is condensed in "Scchs Bretter und zwei Brettchen." Hölderlin's reduction to two boards might have to do with the fundamental structural difference of antiquity and modernity as the difference between unity and duality which has

dominated the reading of antiquity especially since Schiller's opposition of the naive and the sentimental.

23. For an excellent reading and discussion of the configuration of Oedipus and Hamlet, see Julia Reinhard Lupton and Kenneth Reinhard, *After Oedipus: Shakespeare in Psychoanalysis* (Ithaca: Cornell University Press, 1993).

24. Sigmund Freud, *Studienausgabe* (Frankfurt am Main: S. Fischer, 1972), vol. 2: *Die Traumdeutung*, 268.

25. "Es reiche aber, / Des dunkeln Lichtes voll, / Mir einer den duftenden Becher" ("Andenken," vv. 25–27).

26. Charles Baudelaire, *Oeuvres complètes*, Bibliothèque de la Pléiade (Paris: Gallimard, 1976), 2:44–49.

27. Alfred de Musset, "Rolla," in *Poésies Nouvelles* (Paris: Editions Garnier, 1962), 3; Arthur Rimbaud, *Oeuvres* (Paris: Editions Garnier, 1960), 40.

28. Lacan formulates a similar argument about the impossibility of an access to the "gods": "ce champ ne nous est plus guère accessible que du point de vue de l'extérieur, de la science, de l'objectivation, mais ne fait pas partie, pour nous chrétiens, formés par le christianisme, du texte dans lequel se pose effectivement la question. Ce champ des dieux, nous chrétiens, nous l'avons balayé, et c'est justement de ce que nous avons mis à la place qu'il est question ici, à la lumière de la psychanalyse." (Jacques Lacan, *Le séminaire VII: L'éthique de la psychanalyse* [Paris: Editions du Seuil, 1986], 302). As problematic as the emphatic staging of a "nous chrétiens" might seem, it accentuates nevertheless the indelible stamping of our symbolic order by the discourse of Christianity independent of our individual adherences or faith.

29. Baudelaire, *Oeuvres complètes*, 1:114, v. 16.

30. Baudelaire, "Les tentations," 1:308.

31. When Baudelaire, in another poem of *Le spleen de Paris,* offers the Dionysian thyrsus to Liszt (2:335 ff.), the tone seems different, and the Bacchantian celebration points at a *Beauté mystérieuse et passionnée.* But the whole passage stands under the sign of a fundamental sexual ambivalence (which was precisely the mark of the satanic Bacchus of the *Tentations* poem) and links it also to the Lesbians of the *Femmes damnées.* The thyrsos itself, the Dionysian emblem, is radically split in an allegorical reading that separates it into its physical being as a mere dry and hard piece of wood surrounded by flowers and its representation of pure duality.

32. The constellation of Satan with the androgynous phantasy in modernity finds a particularly enigmatic figure in an inscription of Ar-

taud around one of his drawings of Jacques Prevel. On the left side: "L'androgyne rompu reprit l'un et le tenta de l'homme mais c'est [continued on the right side] qu'il tentait de la femme dans le même moment et Satan le feu fut partout." Quoted by Jacques Prevel in *En compagnie d'Antonin Artaud* (Paris: Flammarion, 1994), 149. This edition shows Artaud's portrait drawing of Prevel with part of the inscription on the cover.

33. Benjamin, 1:394.

34. In "Socrates and Tragedy," Nietzsche calls Socrates not only the destroyer of tragedy but also the "herald of science." (Friedrich Nietzsche, *Sämtliche Werke: Kritische Studienausgabe*, ed. Giorgio Colli and Mazzino Montinari (Munich: Deutscher Taschenbuchverlag, 1980), 1:545; hereafter cited parenthetically in the text.

35. Also in the text of *The Birth of Tragedy*, 1:77 ff.

36. Incidentally, the first occurrence of the adjectival form *Dionysisch* in German has been located by Max Baeumer in Goethe's notes for "Pandora": Max Baeumer, "Dialektik und zeitgeschichtliche Funktion des literarischen Topos," in idem, ed., *Toposforschung* (Darmstadt: Wissenschaftl, Buchgesellschaft, 1973), 327.

37. See note 24 above.

CHAPTER 3: TRANSLATIONS OF EROS

1. "Der eingreifendste Unterschied zwischen dem Liebesleben der Alten und dem unsrigen liegt wohl darin, daß die Antike den Akzent auf den Treib selbst, wir aber auf dessen Objekt verlegen. Die Alten feierten den Trieb und waren bereit, auch ein minderwertiges Objekt durch ihn zu adeln, während wir die Triebbetätigung an sich geringschätzen und sie nur durch die Vorzüge des Objektes entschuldigen lassen." Sigmund Freud, *Drei Abhandlungen zur Sexualtheorie,* in *Studienausgabe* (Frankfurt am Main: S. Fischer, 1972), 5:60.

2. "Hölderlins Übersetzungen sind Urbilder ihrer Form; sie verhalten sich auch zu den vollkommensten Übertragungen ihrer Texte als das Urbild zum Vorbild." Walter Benjamin, "Die Aufgabe des Übersetzers," in *Gesammelte Schriften* (Frankfurt am Main: Suhrkamp, 1980), 4:21. All quotations from Benjamin are from this edition.

3. "Dergestalt wird die Sprache zerbrochen, um in ihren Bruchstücken sich einem veränderten und gesteigerten Ausdruck zu leihen" (1:381 ff.).

4. I use the line numbering of the Juntina text that Hölderlin might have used.

5. Charles Segal, *Interpreting Greek Tragedy: Myth, Poetry, Text* (Ithaca: Cornell University Press, 1986), 158.

6. This connotation is emphasized by Gerhard Müller, *Sophokles Antigone* (Heidelberg: Carl Winter, 1967), 173. In contrast to Müller, who intervenes with his emendations in the text with extraordinary dogmatic violence wherever the text does not fit his rather narrow concept of what makes sense (in this case, he categorically rejects *ktêmasi*), we follow here strictly the Juntina version, which seems to have been the basis for Hölderlin's translation. While we are aware of the many textual uncertainties and philological problems in the tradition of the text, we read one particular version precisely as that: as one version in which the unthinkable has been translated.

7. See, e.g., in *Oedipus tyrannos*: v. 40, "kratiston pasin oidipou kara," or v. 1235, "tethnêke Iokastês kara."

8. "When they now see the beauty of the boy and the parts (*merê*) drifting and flowing off from it (which are therefore called desire [*himeros*] . . ."

9. "Das Bild liegt, mit seinen zwei oder drei geheimnisvollen Gegenständen, wie die Apokalypse da, als ob es Youngs Nachtgedanken hätte, und da es, in seiner Einförmigkeit und Uferlosigkeit, nichts, als den Rahm, zum Vordergrund hat, so ist es, wenn man es betrachtet, als ob einem die Augenlider weggeschnitten wären." Heinrich v. Kleist, "Empfindungen vor Friedrichs Seelandschaft," in *Gesamtausgabe* (Munich: Deutscher Taschenbuchverlag, 1964), 5, 61.

10. "Der kühnste Moment eines Taglaufs oder Kunstwerks ist, wo der Geist der Zeit und Natur, das Himmlische, was den Menschen ergreift, und der Gegenstand, für welchen er sich interessirt, am wildesten gegeneinander stehen, weil der sinnliche Gegenstand nur eine Hälfte weit reicht, der *Geist* aber am mächtigsten erwacht, da wo die *zweite Hälfte* angeht. In diesem Momente muß der Mensch sich am meisten festhalten, deswegen steht er auch da am offensten in seinem Karakter." FA 16:412.

11. "Die Nacht oder die Übernachtung, die hier so auffällig hinzugefügt wird, ist an der ersten Stelle mit der Überfahrt über das Meer verbunden, an der zweiten Stelle mit der Überfahrt über die Berge. Ich vermute nun, daß Hölderlin, wie vielleicht auch in einigen seiner wichtigsten Elegien und Hymnen, den Akt des Übersetzens aus dem Griechischen als ein eigentliches Über-Setzen mitreflektiert." Bernhard Böschenstein, *"Frucht des Gewitters": Zu Hölderlins Dionysos als Gott der Revolution* (Frankfurt am Main: Insel, 1989), 40.

12. Theodor W. Adorno, *Ästhetische Theorie*, suhrkamp taschenbuch wissenschaft (Frankfurt am Main: Suhrkamp, 1973), 125 ff.

13. See, e.g., Clytemnestra's attempt to make Cassandra speak in the *Agamemnon* of Aeschylus.

14. Grimm's *Deutsches Wörterbuch* gives as examples: "wer *bei dem berge*, steht auch *an dem berge*; die stadt liegt am Rhein, beim Rhein."

15. Beryl Schlossman has very perceptively suggested the gesture of the prostitute in this slight lifting of the seam: "Pariser Treiben," forthcoming in Christiaan Hart-Nibbrig, ed., *Benjamin Übersetzen* (Frankfurt am Main: Suhrkamp, 1997).

16. Carol Jacobs, "The Monstrosity of Translation: Walter Benjamin's 'The Task of the Translator,'" in *Telling Time: Lévi-Strauss, Ford, Lessing, Benjamin, de Man, Wordsworth, Rilke* (Baltimore: Johns Hopkins University Press, 1993), 141.

Index

Library of Congress Cataloging-in-Publication Data
Nägele, Rainer.
  Echoes of translation : reading between texts / Rainer Nägele.
     p. cm.
  Includes bibliographical references and index.
  ISBN 0-8018-5545-4 (alk. paper)
     1. Translating and interpreting.   I. Title.
P306.N3   1997
809–dc21   96-47331
                                                        CIP